CLASSIFICATION: POETRY

A CIP catalogue record for this book is available from
the British Library.

Printed and bound in Great Britain.

*Cover photograph by courtesy of
the Yorkshire Tourist Board.*

This Hampshire, Berkshire, Buckinghamshire, Oxfordshire,
Bedfordshire, Hertfordshire and Essex edition

ISBN 1-904169-10-4

First published in Great Britain in 2001 by
United Press Ltd
44a St James Street
Burnley
BB11 1NQ
Tel: 01282 459533
Fax: 01282 412679
ISBN for complete set of volumes
1-902803-99-X

www.upltd.co.uk

Visions
in
Verse

Foreword

In my humble opinion the old saying that all things come to those who wait is utter balderdash. I've always believed that you have got to make the effort if you are going to succeed. The poets who feature in this compilation all have that excellent and admirable quality in abundance. They have all made a great personal effort to express themselves, to communicate, and to show that they have confidence in their talent.

That's why I'm so pleased that we at United Press could give these poets a platform upon which to showcase their gift for putting their thoughts into words. Publication in a compilation like this can be, for so many, a major step forward as a writer. It gives encouragement to new poets, fresh hope to experienced ones, and joy to all.

Peter Quinn, Editor

Contents

The poets who have contributed to this volume are listed below, along with the relevant page upon which their work can be found.

56	Jo Badrick	89	Roy Burton
57	Alan Pearn		Amanda Evans
58	Don Friar	90	Yvonne D'Arvigny
59	Ailsa Whitham	91	Jane McLaren
	Harry Horsfall	92	Josephine Nicolson
60	Eddi Newick	93	Ken Clark
	E Denham	94	Patricia Edwins
61	Pat Wood	95	Jane Baker
62	Sharon Folds	96	Patricia Crittenden-
63	David Kennedy		Bloom
64	Tony O'Brien	97	Jean Stewart
	R A Lane	98	E Summers
65	John Garner	99	Michelle Hurley
66	Alison Burgess	100	Nicolette Golding
	Pauline Moulder		Angela Clapham
67	Anne Hadley	101	Erika McCusker
68	Sarah Weyl		Linda Monk
69	Reg C H Baggs	102	Joy K Halfpenny
70	Pauline Waugh		Neil McBride
71	Walter Jennings	103	Angela Barrett
72	A W P Poetry		Helen J Cox
	Linda Butcher	104	Prya Mistry
73	Katrina Day	105	Minnie Fenton
	I Bates	106	Ken Aldred
74	Angela Adams	107	J Booker
75	Marcelle Williams		Sarah Morgan
76	Joan Humphreys	108	Elsie Karbacz
77	Marion Taylor	109	Linda Helm-Manley
	Robert F Belchambers	110	David Lawrence
78	R C Preston	111	D E Flynn
79	R Collins	112	Yolande U Clark
80	Paul Farmer	113	Ana Ahmady
81	Joy O'Brien		James Meek
82	Stewart Harding	114	Micheal Shearer
83	Sandy Rose		Paulene Coe
84	Ron Bird	115	Brandon Penalver
	Enid Skelton	116	Joan Carter
85	R J Hayes		M Elliott
86	Nina Lenton	117	Audrey Wright
87	Suzanne J Webb	118	Pam Williams
	Douglas Darby	119	Wendy Gavin
88	A Marshall	120	Carmel Belcher
	Louise Searl		Aleene Hatchard

121	Nahid Zaman	154	Debby Barnes
122	Janice Thorogood		Sharon Brown
123	Sarah Bidgood	155	William Turton
124	Rebecca Dyer		C Taylor
125	David Evans	156	Lynn Williamson
	Nina McLeod		Mary Barrett
126	Stewart Morton	157	Jennifer Chambers
127	Valerie Smerdon		Christopher Lee
128	Angela Humphrey	158	Pam Farrer
	Catherine May		Vera Saunders
129	Tracey Pugh	159	J F Marshall
130	Teresa Turner		
131	Kean Farrelly		
132	Caroline Mills		
133	Amberley Worton		
134	L Anderson		
135	Dorothy Lawrence		
136	Paul D Walker		
137	Lesley Dearman		
138	Fred Ablitt		
139	Natasha Oakley		
	John Moore		
140	Sarah Nelson		
	Sandra Watson		
141	Clare Collins		
	Daphne Young		
142	Teresa Wood		
143	G W Howe		
144	Irene Robinson		
145	Clive Measey		
146	Pauline Ilott		
	Jessica Salter		
147	Doreen Bowers		
148	M Mayes		
149	A Day		
150	S Bates		
	M Johnson		
151	Constance Cullen		
	Rebecca Wilkinson		
152	Trudie Sullivan		
153	Samantha Rodwell		
	Simon Arms		

LOOKING SOUTH FROM UPPARK

Blue sky drone of some distant plane
Stills, into bird songs with springs light
Green. Some ploughed, March fields fold
Towards the sea; perceive an edge. Leaving
Torrents in the head register remains where
Else in this troubled land. People resolving
Such quiet the lonely vigil.

Chris Pudney, Warsash, Hampshire

WHAT IS LIFE

What is life, can you explain,
when sunshine sometimes turns to rain,
some people cannot ever walk,
while others try, but will not talk,
some are blind, and they can't see,
the love you show when you look at me.

What is life, can you say why,
a new born baby starts to cry,
then there are the people,
who always feel sad,
While others are so happy,
And always being glad.

So thank the Lord for what you've got,
if you have love, you have a lot,
now take you life in both your hands,
and use it while you may,
because it will not last forever,
it will go from you someday.

David William Goosey, Southampton, Hampshire

COME THE QUIET NIGHT

Tumult, turmoil, hurrying day,
Never a moment to think, you say;
Head in a whirl, feet in a rush,
Oh for a minute of soundless hush.
Strange then how one's thoughts abound
In the midst of chores and endless round.
Come the quiet night to set them down
On migrant wings you find they've flown.

Priscilla Noble Mathews, Midhurst, Sussex

HOPING FOR A RAINBOW

a sense of storm warning, a thunderous applause
a sheet of brilliant light, a rush to shut the doors

a scream above the din, a cry for helping hands
a mind of drowning promise, a place where vacant stands

a tumbling down inside, a tide of dormant dreams
a collision course of conscience, a ripping out of seams

a destiny of damage, a recoiled recollection
a piece of person taken, a falsehood for protection

a spark set to attack, a nothing catalyst
a ghost returns to haunt, a demons lips are kissed

a sudden scene revisit, a frightened face remains
a silent wish for freedom, a hope that lasts for change.

David Palmer, Andover, Hampshire

EMPTINESS

My emotions
Swing to and fro
To what? From what?
My emptiness and pain
So many reminders
Each passing day
Reminders that will never capture
Or bring back who I am reminded of.

Margaret Nesbit, Romsey, Hampshire

MY SPECIAL NAN

This is a happy birthday wish,
which I hope you'll never forget,
it will be bright and colourful,
the best you'll have yet.
I wish you a happy birthday,
and hope your wish comes true,
for no-one can be so deserving,
as the person, that is you.
Today is your birthday,
and the years keep rolling by,
but you're still young and beautiful,
a twinkle in my eye.
I hope your day is lovely,
and so special as can be,
then when your day is over,
you can turn your thoughts to me.
The one who loves you dearly,
much more than I can say,
so have a lovely birthday,
in your own sweet special way.

Jessica Louise Thompson, Southampton, Hampshire

SPRING TIME

It's a lovely time of year.
When gardens and flowers come out.
In full bloom with scents and new growth,
And the birds singing their hearts out.
Also busy going back and forward
Building their nests.
Also the sun shines above
Makes one feel alive and kicking.
A lovely time of year.
To start afresh.
And leave the old life behind.

A F Hiscocks, Ludgershall, Hampshire

BEING THREE

Being three
Is everything I thought it would be
It's so much better than two
There's so many more things to do
You can walk a lot more
You can even say things you couldn't before
I feel I'm much bigger
So much more mature
I just can't wait till I'm going on four
I know I'm a little person
But, I'm growing up fast
I'm making the most of it
As I know it won't last
Being three.

Joanna Hall, Southampton, Hampshire

Dedicated to my daughter Janay Amii Hall, who in her tender years inspired me to write Being Three.

DEPRESSION

Black, black, and still more black.
Long, long tunnel of nothing that leads nowhere.
Walk, walk, walk, not even seeing an end,
Regardless of knowing I cannot get there anyway.

Shadows behind,
Shadows in front,
So big they just don't matter any more.
Steep, steep sides, impossible to climb.
Deep, deep sides.
Heavy shoes, dragging, sagging.
Lonely, lonely, desperately lonely,
Yet shunning company, knowing that the disease is catching.

Hating having nothing to do,
But not wanting anything to do,
The light too dim to go on,
Yet not dark enough to stop.
Just straight, no bend.
No beginning, no end.

Penelope Daly, New Milton, Hampshire

Born in London **Penelope Daly** enjoys embroidery, patchwork, beading and writing children's stories. "I am an only child of working parents so my imagination helped me to fill my solitary world," she remarked. "My work is influenced by all my life experiences and the people I meet and my style is usually a great deal happier than this poem. I would like to be remembered as someone who loved a lot and was loved a lot." Aged 61 she is a retired teacher. She is widowed with two children and two grandchildren. "The person I would most like to meet is my mother so we could talk about all the things we didn't discuss when she was here," said Penelope. "I have written around 50 poems and had a couple published. I have also had 2 children's books published."

UNTITLED

Once there was a man named Paul
Who went to a fancy dress ball
He said "just for fun,
I'll dress up as a bun"
But a dog ate him up in the hall.

Melissa Mayer, Kidlington, Oxfordshire

DREAMS

If I should close my eyes and slowly start to dream,
I'd imagine wondrous things for instance paddling in a
steam.
I'd climb the tallest mountains and I'd swim from shore to
shore,
Things that seem impossible I'd conquer by the score.

I'd ride horses through dense forests and saunter across
the hills,
I'd drive cars at speed and even spin the wheels.
I'd play football with the boys and netball with the girls,
I'd go panning with gold prospectors and search oyster
shells for pearls.

For this is how to enjoy life simply in one's dreams,
To find gold at the foot of the rainbow and walk on shad-
ows from moonbeams.
But reality is quite different and life's not all it seems,
So just live a life of fantasy by hanging on to dreams.

Carol Edney, Waterlooville, Hampshire

MY TROUBLED MIND

I am lost in the wilderness of my mind
Searching for a way, looking for a sign
Though, I have to confess
I am struggling to find
Any peace, for my troubled mind

I am standing still, with time
My life now a desert
No life at all
Nothing to look forward for
E'en though I held out a hand
My life now, a wasteland

You see, memories for me
Of days gone bye
They are so clear, almost redefined
For the love that I felt for you
Way back when
It is so troubling my mind
For I still feel the love for you
That I did back then

Andrew Dodsworth, Catherington, Hampshire

AUTUMN

Autumn, the season of hibernation,
For the gradual cessation of summer,
The young animals now adults,
The leaves descending in a dazzling array of colour,
The evenings diminishing,
Nature hurriedly preparing
For its greatest physical test.

Oliver Edwards, Havant, Hampshire

WHEN APRIL COMES

High in the Lammermuirs
Waiting for spring;
Shepherds are wondering
What April may bring

Watching through winter
In snow, fog and frost,
Ready to seek for
A ewe that is lost.

Indoors to the barn,
The flock settles to wait,
Primroses greet the sun
Near the farm gate.

Out on the hillside
When winter storms pass,
White lambs like daisies
Bloom on the green grass.

Beryl Louise Penny, Brockenhurst, Hampshire

THE HOUSE

In summertime I will not come
To the house that you called home in Goldington,
Where two tall fir trees linger yet,
Inside the brick wall there so red.

For you have gone so far away.
Yet ever near you will stay.
And though my memory sometimes fades;
Some little thing, some slight remark,
A distant bell will start to ring,
And I'll remember everything.

And sadness for an instant comes
To put a cloud beside the sun,
And sadly I must turn away,
For life it daily must be run,
Against an ever setting sun.

D Grant, Southampton, Hampshire

Born in London **Daphne Grant** started writing poetry in
1982. "My work is influenced by great writers and artists
and my style is straightforward," she said. "I would like to
be remembered as an appreciator of great prose and good
English." Aged 67 she has an ambition to write poetry as
good as some of her idols. She is married to Peter and they
have one child. "I have written several poems and had
many of them published," she said. "I have also written an
article on T E Lawrence and my biggest fantasy is to lecture
on Joseph Conrad."

DOVER 1916

The pounding could be heard across the water
As the cannons performed their mighty slaughter;
For, with every burst, life was lost
And who could count the human cost,
As the distant thundering rolled
And the passing bells sadly tolled?

Inwardly, her anxiety burned
Awaiting the moment he returned.

Shane Lloyd Price, Ryde, Hampshire

THE LABYRINTH

She made my life beautiful
She was its purpose,
And now she's gone.
I am empty, my days unfilled.
Time, once flying with her
Now clings heavy,
Like an unwanted friend.
I am lonely for myself,
Watch myself decline,
Wander without purpose,
Catch myself at odds
With where I am
Knowing nothing
Of where I've been.
But, wherever I am without her,
Lost in the labyrinth
Of me.

T Hennessy, Winchester, Hampshire

THE NIGHT

For the night is my realm
It gives me strength to fight my foes
It gives shadow to hide from thoughts that know how to
destroy me
I control darkness
For it gave me life
And I give it meaning.

Anthony Oliver, Gosport, Hampshire

THE CHILD'S PUSHCHAIR

The horrific picture flashed up on the TV screen
of a vicious bombing on a village scene,
There, stood in the centre was a child's pushchair
Nothing else except rubble in a picture so obscene.

The picture moved on screaming of injured people filled the
air.
Some searching for loved ones, some blown to pieces in
this awful war
what is the sense of it all? Always the innocent and the
poor
are the victims of fanatical dreams of the so called
religious pair.

The little child thankfully survived, blown on to soft dirt
just one of many so dreadfully hurt
Let them keep the pushchair standing proud
a monument to remind us that miracles are still allowed.

Kathleen Collins, Alton, Hampshire

ALWAYS

In the spring I will lick buds
And the taste will be yours,
In summer streams the light
Is caught as by your smile,
The autumn chestnuts have the same
Warm brown depth as your eyes,
For you winter will have no cold
For I will kindle these things
And always be your hearth,
Steady and all aflame.

Mihangel Evans, Milton Keynes, Buckinghamshire

For Bibi, who makes it all possible.

SWEET BELLY BUTTON

I'm a belly button eater
I can think of nothing sweeter
Cooked and seasoned to a turn
Not one belly button would I burn

As yours is ripe for eating
I will have, no more bleating
I will get my belly button remover
It's a special attachment to hoover

It will not hurt a lot
But it will leave a spot
I'll give you a big plaster
So it will heal faster

Peter Ranson, Ryde, Isle Of Wight

THE BLUE PLANET

The blue planet as earth is aptly named
Shows seas and oceans as it spins through space
And whirling clouds forever changing course
To give a different look to Gaia's face.
And from our viewpoint there are skies of blue;
The lakes that mirror skies; the shadows deep
That mark the snow; bluebirds and butterflies
And coastal rocks on which blue mussels creep.

So many lovely things are tinted blue.
The magic misty shapes of distant hills;
A camp fire's curling smoke, the darkening night,
And flowers whose charm and welcome presence thrills.
The fragrant bluebells carpeting the woods;
Forget me nots and gentians, chicory;
The bright germander speedwells, harebells, flax.
To troubled hearts they bring tranquility.

Mavis Vigay, Waterlooville, Hampshire

A DAY REMEMBERED

I woke to hear the water lapping
At my feet and rose to meet
The sound of gulls' wings flapping
Upon the damp, mist laden air.

I heard above me, soft and clear
The thud of sails raised to bear
The first, fresh breeze of dawn,
And shaking sand from sleepy eyes
I raised my face to salt sea spray,
To watch the ocean touch the skies,
Under another heaven and a remembered day.

Elizabeth Cahillane, Petersfield, Hampshire

ANOTHER MARTHE

To see your figure,
Alabaster,
Pure, unblemished,
Clean,
Shimmering with desire,
Gliding out the shower,
A fantastical, unicorn dream.
Bathed in gold,
At first I didn't recognise,
You were swallowed by the sheen,
Then you tore your body from the decorated surface,
A majestic Venus scene.
You walked out from the body of Olympia,
With your eyes positioned at a glance,
Why couldn't you look me in the eye,
Why do I make you feel so enhanced?

Rachel Magdeburg, High Wycombe, Buckinghamshire

AN OLD FASHIONED GIRL

I like it when men call me 'dear'
Or touch their hats when I draw near
I love it when they open doors
So I can enter first, of course.

I even like men whistling me
From building sites or up a tree,
And standing up on crowded trains
Or sharing brollies when it rains.

It's not 'politically correct'
At least that's what folk say.
But I've decided to deflect
Enjoy it while I may.

Frances Heckler, Ryde, Isle Of Wight

Born in Birmingham **Frances Heckler** enjoys photography, gardening, music, art and writing. "I began writing poetry at school," she pointed out. "English was my best subject, followed closely by art. My work is influenced by everyday life and funny or silly things that happen and my style is easy reading and often amusing. Frances is a journalist and is married to Keith. "I have written about 40 poems and had several published," she said. Frances is a former magazine editor and was involved in public relations for several years.

PARIS

You are the echo of something far from here,
Yet near, like an early morning breeze.
A symphony of visionary rhymes and you appear,
A Dionysus in the chaos of my renaissance dreams.
Dreams of envy, gluttony and sloth and fear
Of missing any part of it yet not dare
To take your cold hand and let it fall,
As you leave me without one word of comfort or farewell.

Michele Busk, Cowes, Isle Of Wight

Dedicated to Crispin Groom who shared my Paris experience and is the subject of this poem.

Michele Busk said: "I was born and brought up in Hampshire. After a year in America I trained and worked in Oxford for five years. I also worked abroad in Bulgaria, France and the Middle East as a secretary/translator and then returned to London. I moved to the Isle of Wight in order to devote more time to writing and art. I began writing poetry at school and I'm currently working on a novel and a collection of short stories. Poems come out of the blue. My life is my inspiration and I enjoy painting, sailing, skiing, music and travel and hope one day to be a published author."

ODE TO SPRINGTIME

O hedgy-hog, and rolly-pog, and things that go all nutty
The spring has come, frolic in the sun, on legs that act
quite potty
The time of year when fancies nearly drive us slightly batty
And nature's new frock and her frolicking stock
Are looking blooming pretty.

Gwyneth Rushton, Selborne, Hampshire

LIFE IS LIKE A ROLLER COASTER

Life never runs smoothly,
riding on a roller coaster;
Hey. baby, what are you doing to me,
you were put here to try and test;
but now I have rhythm to tease,
Like you I lift your soul to please;
Sending me higher than clouds,
Along with depths of watery crevasses;
Come join the harmony and reach new heights,
Riding on a roller coaster;

When in dreams higher than the sky,
Rocket round Mars and back;
Yet with feet firmly planted,
Go sailing and dive feeding rays with delight,
My paradise location comes around,
In spasms of laughter made in a heaven I know;
To love this moment lost in time flight,
To bloom with splendour caught in a web of   candyfloss;
Here we go again erotic eurythmics
Riding on a roller coaster.

Phillip Clarke, Freshwater, Isle Of Wight

DAD

I think you are there looking down on me
I think you are there although I can't see
I think you are there and you know my pain
I think you are there and you feel the same
I think you are there and remember the fun
Of the days gone by when we were young
I think you are there and you share our love
I think you are there in heaven above.

Maxine Piggott, Buckingham, Buckinghamshire

SPRINGTIME IN HAMPSHIRE

The rolling hills of Hampshire
Aglow with hoare frost in winter

Even snow at times, to keep seeds warm
Come springtime green shoots appearing
All manner of wonderful colours

Tractors busy with life
Everything is suddenly moving
One can feel spring, almost summer, in the air
Lambs are gambolling away on new round grass

Shoots on the forest trees are opening wide
Birds preening themselves and building nests
Looking so carefree and happy

The deer are prancing about
The ponies shed their winter coats
All getting ready for a glorious summer

V Willan, Andover, Hampshire

THE JOURNEY

The wheels roll,
The miles pass by.
I look up aimlessly.
The sun fills my eye
The fresh morning air
Touches my face.
As I gaze up
into distant space.

Grace Major, Milton Keynes, Buckinghamshire

SEASONS

The seasons of the year go on,
We cannot change their time or form,
Each one in turn brings joy in views,
Nature lives, fades, its growth renews.
Glorious colours of autumn harvest,
Fill our countryside with nature's best.
Trees with all their variegated leaves
Gives such spectacle of colour schemes,
Ferns curl up their faded frons
Turning shades from green to bronze.
Winter's shorter days and nights,
Cool darkness somehow warmed by lights.
When moonlight glows across the world,
A cold, brilliant orb unfurls.
Onset of winter is felt by everything,
Crisp air, high winds, little joy to bring.
But each year nature's beauty is unfurled,
Rest awhile, observe, enjoy this wondrous world.
Warm summer days bring heartfelt joy,
A new energy to everything employs.

Pamela Benham, Southsea, Hampshire

MY DARLING

My days are filled with thoughts of you
Of all the sweet and tender things you'd do
Of dreams we shared, and those that were fulfiled.
Love so deep, so true, so strong will not be stilled.

I feel you everywhere I go.
You're close beside me still, I know.
Your strength still ebbs and flows to me.
Your presence shines through everything I see.

I cannot say I really miss you, dear
Your love surrounds me and your words are near
Guiding, whispering, showing me the way.
My darling, please stay close to me today.

When life gets tough and I feel small and weak.
Breath love on me, tender words please speak.
Into my soul, into my mind and heart.
Until we're together, no more to part.

Maureen Van-der-Lowen, Buckingham, Buckinghamshire

Written for my husband, Norm who died suddenly. His memory forever loved and cherished by all his family.

Born in London **Maureen Van-der-Lowen** enjoys reading, writing, sewing and spending time with her family. "I started writing poetry as a young girl," she remarked. "I always committed my deepest feeling to paper so that I could better express human emotions. My work is influenced by life, people and deep, inexpressible feelings and my style is empathetic and emotional. I would like to be remembered as a helpful, caring person who influenced people's lives for the good." Aged 62 she is a teacher who has written children's stories and hundreds of poems, although this is the first one she has attempted to published. She is a widow with three children and six grandchildren.

LIVE FOR THE DAY

Live for the day,
For life is strange.
There is no use in trying
To arrange ahead,
For we know not
What may come
In future years: Nor of
All the tears,
To yet be shed.
Fear and dread breeds sorrow:
So think not of tomorrow:
For to be of moderate health
Means so much more than wealth:
Why waste time anticipating:
When happiness may be
Waiting only around the corner:
and all the grey may turn to gold;
Another day.

Gaenor Spratley, Milton Keynes, Buckinghamshire

TIDE

My keeping place has a channel
Lined with pebbles, promises
I have rubbed it, deep
With the current and movement of life's gentle sleep.
Waves eddy behind me, come to stand position,
Whispering release, untangling my fingers
In time's requisition.
Release, release
And I am transparent here, clean and alive
Rest, peace
Sigh
Drift
Sigh.

Fiona Watson, Stanstead, Essex

TERRORIST

Staring out of the window at the grey skies,
The rain spits on the pavement, I can't take it.
I slouch on the sofa and shut my blurry eyes,
Fierce hot tears roll down my cheeks.
Outside, the sounds of happy children echo,
Splashing and squealing in the puddles.
I remember when I was young and innocent,
Floating upturned milk bottle tops in puddles.
I leave, children's happy squeals burning in my ears,
Soon they would squeal for another reason.
I wish I didn't have to do what I'm about to,
But it has to be done, it's down to me.
Tomorrow morning I will make headline news,
Appalling a devastated nation. It's down to me.

Catherine Howes, Colchester, Essex

THE WAR MEMORIAL

In a corner of Luxembourg
is a narrow half forgotten road
running alongside the edge of a wood.
A small sign in the village
says "War Memorial".
An arrow points into the dark
mysterious forest ahead.
The track winds it way among the
trees which are tall and
close together. The daylight
is obscured by the heavy foliage.
Where can the memorial be?
Suddenly shafts of sunlight break through.
Ahead is a clearing and there it is
the remains of an aircraft
scattered across the forest floor,
left exactly where it crashed.
It is so silent, not a leaf moves.
A fitting memorial to the brave
Allied airmen and one I shall never forget.

Gillian Whittome, Gerrards Cross, Buckinghamshire

MEMORIES

Our life is full of memories
Tucked away behind closed doors
Stored in small compartments
Of our mind, but there are flaws.

As fleeting memories escape
Sometimes they're hard to grasp,
Leaving ghostly feelings behind
Of some time in our past.

We all have special memories
That no one else can share
Perhaps some quiet time together
With someone no longer there.

Life without our memories
Would be a barren one
Imagine never reminiscing
Of the time when you were young.

As we all get older
Perhaps unable to go out
We rely upon our memories
To know what life was all about.

T Jones, Buckingham, Buckinghamshire

*I dedicate this poem to my late husband Ken, with happy
thoughts of all our years spent together.*

MY FRIEND

If one thought of me, can stay,
Forever in your heart,
Sincere with words, I'll always say,
Why did we have to part?,
But, if you should ever need a friend,
Through all the years to come,
One word of "Sorry", I can send,
Let not my lips be dumb,
And yet, we're still apart,
And you do not seem to care,
There's still a place, within my heart,
That none, but you can share.

John Harper-Smith, Buckinghamshire

ALWAYS AND NEVER

Never judge a book by its cover
Never compare one person with another.
Never live a lie 'cos believe me when you die,
you'll see judgement for your sister and your brother.

Always be true to yourself
If you can't be true to anyone else.
The spirit world are spying
I know you think I'm lying
but the body didn't work by itself.

Actions speak louder than words,
So make sure when it's said it is heard.
Spiritual beings know your thoughts
Human beings will be caught,
So by plastic friends please don't be lured.

Delvena Constant, Ebbes, Oxfordshire

RIVER OF LIFE

Silken dark tresses flowing down,
down from the source.
Covering many miles along the way
sometimes deep and sinister,
sometimes shallow and sharp.

Flowing over rocky places
flowing over smooth sand-beds
until, years later they tumble
into a curling white waterfall

Power and wisdom
meet at this point and then
when their reasoning has
run its course,
they release the tresses,
now white with wandering,
into the stillness of the lake.

Dawn Cook, Headington, Oxfordshire

IN THE GARDEN

Dad is in the garden,
putting veggies in the ground,
birds are singing around us,
it is a lovely sound.

Grandad is in the greenhouse,
potting up new seeds,
Mum is at the flowerbed,
pulling up the weeds.

My brother has a pocket of bugs,
a huge worm is in his hand,
and my sister has her bucket and spade,
she's making castles in the sand.

My dog is in the garden,
he's playing with his ball,
and I am climbing up a tree,
so must be careful not to fall.

Karen Taplin, Henley-on-Thames, Oxfordshire

KEYBOARD PLAYER

Simon, Simon, hidey me,
You follow every improvisational tree
Branching off in all directions,
Changing key unmercifully.
We can scarcely keep pace
In your scalectic race
Over old photographic notes,
In black and white, in lightening bolts
Of jolting shock waves,
Sounds to force the overwrought
To hurry, tear their figurative hair
For figurative birds nests.

Diane Burrow, Witney, Oxfordshire

SOMETHING BRILLIANT

Gently gliding, something brilliant came one day
Soft and light
Burnished and dazzling
Strong and bold
Warm and melting
Inviting, inviting
Heard it breathe
Felt it move
Tried to touch it
Wanted to embrace it
Thought I caught a wisp
Thought I had it in my grasp
Missed
Passed me by
Gliding
Gone.

Sara Jane Gross, Potters Bar, Hertfordshire

MY GRANDSON

As soft as silk, like golden corn his hair,
Eyes a pale blue touched with green,
Sparkling with mischief, then serene,
With lashes long, warm skin like thistledown,
Who could resist his early charms?
His baby ways bring sunshine to my autumn days,
Then with his tiny hand in mine,
I feel at peace, that life is good,
All grandmamas will surely know,
Just how I feel, I love him so.

Kathleen Edmond, Wallingford, Oxfordshire

THE MEMORY BOX

The nurse comes
to give my mother a blanket bath.
She seems to shrink after each washing.
When we lift her to change the sheets
she is a little bird of bones.
I want to cup her in my hands
and croon reassuring words.
Her skin is thin as tissue paper.
She is using it to wrap memories for me -
'Do you remember when?'
We pour over old photos, fingers brushing.
Two things we were never good at,
sharing and touching.
Eyes bright with pain and morphine
my little mother works against time
to fill my memory box,
lining it with the soft moss of her love.
Death will put the final lid on it.

Carolyn Garwes, Shillingford, Oxfordshire

DAISY

Close I cling to the awakening earth,
Petals open to receive the warming sun,
Revealing my heart of gold within,
The rays of sunlight give me birth.

My numbers are scattered far and wide,
Woven into chains by many a child,
But sadly cut down before my time
Whenever the grass grows wild.

But, please, just leave me lying here
Upon my bed of luscious green,
And I, amongst all flowers,
Am fit to be their queen.

Justine Ann Booth, Woodstock, Oxfordshire

JOAN

How do I love thee? Let me count the ways
I love thee as I love thy home made jam
I love thy sunday roast, especially lamb
From yonder kitchen wafts a heady haze
Surpassing that of Raymond Blanc in praise
Thy tender love like honey-glazed ham
My heart could never turn to thoughts of spam
Thy mighty turkey dinner how it weighs
Thy coconut cake springy spongy bliss
All iced in pink worth far more than a kiss
Each visit, flavours new, like filoed fig
I'm honoured deeply playing guinea pig
Thy culinary talents plain to see
I think I love thy cooking more than thee.

Diana Moore, Oxford, Oxfordshire

LOOKING BACK

Now the wind is cold and the skies are grey
Let's look back to a sunny day.
Do you remember the sun on high
That gazed on us from a clear blue sky?
I can remember a cabin small
Perched on a terrace 'neath pines so tall
And through them the softest breeze blew
And 'neath them wild flowers of every hue.
Do you remember the olive and vine,
In the days when we feasted on bread and wine?
I can remember ripe cherries so red,
Black olives and cheese with crusty bread.
Do you remember the song of the birds,
The gay butterflies and the wild boars you heard?
Does the land yield and grow at a pace?
I'll always remember that wonderful place,
And when the wind blows and snow's on the ground
I'll dream of the sunshine that spread all around.

Jean English, Wallingford, Oxfordshire

ASHES

A cold taste of ashes in my mouth
from the funeral pyres inside of me
the cold stiffened corpses
of my dreams, my hopes, my heart
smouldering on the cold fire
that sends a chill through my veins
the smell sickens me
nauseated I see the world spin past
unable to stop it
unable to get on
I turn away to attend the wake.

Lise Hvalkof, Broxbourne, Hertfordshire

FIRST IMPRESSIONS

The tiny beauty spot
at the corner of your mouth
and your cheeks' rich blush.

The peacock-blue dust
around your burnt amber eyes,
the brunette pile on

the back of your head,
careless but right. And how
could I forget your

strong, firm, shapely legs,
made for dancing? The glimpses
brushing my mind's eye.

Jonathan Doering, Witney, Oxfordshire

NO APOLOGIES

I apologise
For not loving you enough
Not giving you the flowers
And not whispering 'love you' more often.

I apologise
For not being able to comfort you enough
When you were tired and exhausted
And not being there to hold you.

I apologise
For the lost moments when the moon was up
Stars were twinkling and during the sunset
When walking with you, I did not kiss you.

I apologise
For being unhappy for trivial things.
For not being fully appreciative
Of your generosity and your kindness,

But I do not apologise
For loving you with all my heart
And my soul. Being forever grateful
For your affection and your friendship.

Somen Sen, Croxley, Hertfordshire

BITTER OCEAN

A sea of hearts swells
and bursts itself against the stone wall of your shore.

And hearts fall back, broken and bloodless
upon the blood of those that went before.

So that all your harbours may be filled with claret;
that you might gently sip your victory
reclining upon a calm sea
with dashing hearts no more.

Christopher James Davia, Stevenage, Hertfordshire

Christopher Davia said: "I am 42 and single, presently
doing research into the brain at Carnegie Mellon University
in Pittsburgh, USA. My hobbies are reading, chess, problem
solving, crosswords and socialising. My ambition is to con-
tribute to man's understanding of himself and his relation-
ship to the universe. I have written 25 poems, two short
stories and a hypothesis entitled 'Minds, Brains, Chaos and
Catalysis an ontological approach to the mind/brain prob-
lem.' Shakespeare, Herman Melvile and personal experience
have influenced my work. I would like to be remembered
affectionately and for my sense of humour."

MOONLIGHT

Oh, mysterious light of the night
Casting ghostly shadows over the sleeping earth,
Silent clouds pass slowly across your face,
And are banished away by the gentle winds of time.

Oh, magical light of the heavens
Shine on us mortals forever while we sleep,
May your glowing light be always there,
Guiding us through the dark nights of our lives.

Olive Mitchell, Kings Langley, Hertfordshire

Olive Mitchell said: "I have only ever written one or two poems mostly for my own enjoyment and was delighted when my poem 'Moonlight' was chosen to be included in this book. It was looking at a beautiful full moon one night that inspired me to write the poem. I have one son and one daughter, both married, and three grandchildren, my husband Ken sadly died in 1979. Now retired, I am an avid reader. I love music and also like to do cross-stitch, embroidery and, who knows, I might even pen another poem."

A DATE WITH DEATH

No, not tonight, I'm washing my hair
As a date with you I just can't bear
Save your breath, I wouldn't bother
Arrangements made to meet another
Now don't you cry, please understand
That I can never be your man
There's plenty more fish in the sea
So leave behind your thoughts of me
It's nothing personal, you're not my type
I have a lover and her name is life.

Ian Parrett, Watford, Hertfordshire

A MUSICAL LIFE

You spent your childhood
Frolicking with the allegro of youth
Through the pizzicato of chaos that was
Your adolescence.

The tempo quickened
In young adulthood
And the harmonies crunched
In triumphant splendour.

As life played on,
The rubato began.
The legato melody portrayed
Happiness and contentment.

Looking forward to those
Mellow tones of retirement,
And the andante of old age.

Bethan Lee, Hoddesdon, Hertfordshire

MY MUM

You know I love you very much
that is why I have written this poem for such
A wonderful mum
for now and to come.
Thanks for all your good advice
It was definitely more than twice.
You always make me smile,
Every once in a while,
You would tell me funny things,
Like how birds got their wings.
I'm glad I have a mum like you
to share things with and sing to.
Even if you don't like what I'm wearing
You are still very caring.

Sarah Cooke, Welwyn Garden City, Hertfordshire

I dedicate this to my Mum who encourages me to never give up, despite what I put her through.

Born in Welwyn Garden City **Sarah Cooke** enjoys music, football and reading. "I started writing poetry four years ago," she remarked. "My work is influenced by my late father's books and I would like to be remembered as someone who enjoys life and never stops talking." Aged 11 she is a schoolgirl with an ambition to be a specialised child's nurse at Great Ormond Street hospital. Sarah has written many poems and had several published. "My biggest fantasy is to sing on stage with Eminem and the person I would most like to be for a day is Julia Roberts. I would love to meet Tony Adams who is a great footballer for Arsenal and England."

SUBURBAN MELANCHOLY

The semi-rural squire,
slave of half an acre
of flint and stubborn clay,
rested on his spade so hard
it broke in two.
Got wot the garden, cried he,
mangling the old poet.
Within his easy view
a robin delicately shat
and a worm theatrically writhed.
Through all this natural frenzy
he mutely tried to meditate,
while all around inside his head
whined passages from string quartets.

Donald Cameron, Bedmond, Hertfordshire

Donald Cameron said: "For a good many years I have been writing short rhymes and other short pieces, mainly for my own amusement. During the last two or three years our local paper, The Villager, has fairly regularly published my contributions. The tone of these has generally, been quirky, although I have now and then revealed something of myself. I have no ambitions as a writer, except perhaps to build a regular readership locally for my contributions."

THE COCKEREL

When we're woken up at dawn
by crowing cocks that greet the morn,
our sleeping brains so rude disturbed,
bring forth expletives of that bird.
A bird that likens to no other,
piercing calls we'd like to smother.
But oh so proud, its strutting gait,
shimmering feathers looking great,
cause one to stop and gaze in awe,
as this big bird is total law
to all the hens that dwell in coups,
whose destiny might end in soups.
Or stripped down bodies roasted brown,
chewed and relished, swallowed down.
Glad to say the cockerel's fate
lies more in service to his mate.
So, not for table this bright bird,
he'll keep on crowing, he must be heard.

Ruth Vickers, Kings Langley, Hertfordshire

SPECIAL FRIEND

You made me feel special.
And you made me feel loved.
You taught me how to smile.
And you made my heart skip a beat.

You shared with me stories.
Of love lost and found.
And you shared with me ideas, of how friendship could
last.

Somehow you've found your way
Back into my heart
I hope you won't give up on me.
As I've done on you.

It's sad to think that you won't even
Know how I feel for you.
A love untarnished, so simple and true.
Always, it would remain hidden in my heart
A real loss of friendship on your part.

Lory Centena, Stevenage, Hertfordshire

TALKING HANDS

When you start you're all fingers and thumbs
the words you think will never come
A few lessons later the embarrassment goes
And there a few signs you begin to know.

You first learn your name
Practising again and again
Then just as you think you've got there, you've won
They go and ask you to sign your second one.

You spell it out slow and clear
You miss a digit then oh dear.
Poor old Fred
Is not ill, he's dead.

Still never mind, there always time
To practice a little more.

Sally Waldman, Royson, Hertfordshire

Sally Waldman said: "I have been writing poetry for three years and this is my third poem to be published. My poems are personal experiences that link me to individuals or events that make an impression on me. I started signing classes to learn a language but came away learning about a whole way of life. I have been married to Roger for 11 years and have two children, Josef aged nine and Bethany aged five. I have started college as a mature student studying psychology, sociology and human biology with the hopes and ambitions of going to university."

BUTTERFLIES

Thoughts are butterflies that flutter
into the garden of the mind.

They hover in the air
and for a fleeting moment
you can touch them
before they fly away.

Sometimes, on balmy summer days,
they settle on a rose so you can dream.

The poet chases,
catches them in a net,
and calls them inspiration.

Joyce Walker, Borehamwood, Hertfordshire

SEAGULL

On virgin wings I learnt to fly
Feathers unfurled against the sky
The earth spun round, and down fell I
So this is what it is to die

My mother's body halts my fall
Graceful eyes have seen it all
A skillful nudge, a wingtip raised
Panic fades, I bask in praise

Now I swoop and glide and soar
The grounded cliffs are far below
Mama watch me, I can fly
Hear my heartsong fill the sky.

Ahi Wheeler, Letchworth, Hertfordshire

FAKE

There once was a girl I used to know
Her stunning looks, made quite a show
With long blonde hair, and a knee-trembling smile
She stood out more than a mile.

She seemed so nice, generous and kind
But I never knew what lurked behind
She snarled and bit, and wouldn't yield
She's responsible for the way I feel.

I Pennell, Hemel Hempstead, Hertfordshire

THE GRANDFATHER CLOCK

The grandfather clock stands in the hall
So elegant and tall. He tells the time, each hour that
chimes
His pendulum swings as he unwinds.
He has never been known to tell the wrong time
Children count on their fingers every beat of his chimes
They know when he rings at six o' clock that this means
bedtime
Sadly they climb the wooden stairs, kneel and say their
prayers
Prayers over, they jump into bed pulling covers up to their
heads.
They like to lay and listen to the gentle tock of their old
friend,
Grandfather clock.

Irene Hartley, Hertford, Hertfordshire

2001

Here it is, two thousand and one...
Despite the strange new date,
The sun still shines on,
As it has always done,
And the bumblebees
Inspect the geranium flowers,
Bright purple-blue,
As they have always done,
To my recollection,
And will, I hope, always do.

Hugh Loxdale, Batford, Hertfordshire

Hugh Loxdale said: "I was born in Horley, Surrey. I started writing poetry, especially on natural history themes, in my late teens. I have two poetry books published, 'The Eternal Quest' (1988; Merlin Books Ltd) and 'Blue Skies in Tuscany' (2000; Minerva Press) and am presently preparing two further volumes for publication. The poem '2001' explores our perception of time, suggesting that the millennial date change is a purely human cultural one rather than meaningful as such, especially in terms of evolutionary changes in the natural world. These generally occur over much longer time spans, and often go unperceived until studied."

LIFE TODAY

The world is a strange place,
We rush everywhere to get nowhere,
We work all our lives in pursuit of what?
A house, a car, nice holidays.
Only then to want, a bigger house, a bigger car, more holidays.
We save all our money,
Only to have someone else spend it when we are no more.
Life is not fair but it was never meant to be,
Sometimes it is the pits,
And then sometimes nothing in the world can better it.
Do you stop and listen?
Really listen to the leaves rustling and the robin singing.
You think you see everything,
But actually in reality you see nothing at all.
You come in with nothing,
And you go out the same way.
Rich, poor, black, white, male or female.
This law applies to all living things.
So live, live life,
It starts today.

Anita Whyman, Royston, Hertfordshire

NO MORE RESPONSIBILITY

Once all my chicks have flown, what shall I do
When I no longer have them to see to?
I won't have to make sure they're out of bed,
I could lie in 'til dinner time instead.
Won't have to lay in snacks for them to crunch,
Won't have to check they've packed tomorrow's lunch
There won't be endless washing any more,
One load each day instead of three or four,
The freezer and the fridge will not be crammed,
The airing cupboard be no longer jammed,
For once I can spread out on my settee,
And watch just what I want on my TV.
Won't have to check alarms are set and wound,
Necessity because they sleep so sound,
Won't get a goodnight cuddle and a kiss,
A very precious thing I'm going to miss.
They won't be living with me any more,
And I am going to miss them, that's for sure.

Jo Badrick, Tring, Hertfordshire

Dedicated to Claire, Charlotte and Paul, my family for twenty five years past and for always, with my love.

Born in Edgware **Jo Badrick** enjoys crocheting blankets for charity. "I started writing poetry in my teens because I liked finding rhyming words and telling a story at the same time," she explained. "My work is influenced by my Christian faith and I can't abide poetry which doesn't scan or rhyme. I would like to be remembered as someone who wrote truthfully about what she saw and how she felt." Aged 58 she is a foster mother and is widowed. "My only child died at birth, hence the fostering," she said. "I have written hundreds of poems but had none published until now."

SATIN BLUE

Beneath blue satin, pink roses and bows,
a little girl's mind begins to dream.

She's in her fantasy world far away
where nobody but her has been.

She's a princess of space from the human
race a million light years from home.

On a snow white pony she crosses the
sky, passing silver moons all alone.

Perfumed with sweetness, earthly and
true, she sips her Venus champagne
as she sets free the stars in her
galaxy of satin blue.

In her magical world of make believe,
she dreams the light years away between
Jupiter and Mars and a million stars,
only to return someday.

Alan Pearn, Harpenden, Hertfordshire

FAITH

Like shafts of light, piercing the dark
Like a matured tree, losing its bark.
Like a teenager, leaving home
Forging forward, evermore to roam.

A time to relax, to be still with God
A time to repent, to spare the rod,
Remembering the happy times, now that you are alone
Remembering the children, coming home.

Waiting hoping, testing your faith
Talking to God, feeling so safe,
He will be there waiting, arms open wide
He will heal you, he will provide.

Listen closely, then you will hear
The Lord's sweet message, loud and clear.
Have faith, have patience, with a heart full of love,
And you will find healing, in his eternal love.

Don Friar, Harpenden, Hertfordshire

Don Friar said;; "I have been published in several anthologies. My work is influenced by the people and places around me, I often get inspiration during the middle of the night. I was born in my grandmother's house during the war, in a village in Hertfordshire, called Colney Heath. I am married and have fostered six children, not being able to have children of my own. I enjoy writing, art and I am writing a short story at the moment. A copy of 'A Touch of Verse' can be obtained from Clive Hill, 21 High Street, Kimpton, Hertfordshire, SG4 8QN, priced at £3 (plus £1.50 p&p) per copy."

A NEW MORNING

Peacefully tranquil,
the air is serene,
awaiting a moment,
for day to be seen.

Eastwardly rising
the sun we await,
for dawn is upon us,
we anticipate.

Ailsa Whitham, Radlett, Hertfordshire

FAREWELL TO THE OLD YEAR

I heard it,
In the faint
Rustling sound
Of leaves falling
From near naked trees;
I saw it,
In the look
Of lingering
Lifeless blooms
And dried berries;
I felt it,
In the cold
Sleet laced
December wind;
And I wondered
At the beauty
Of the dying year,
Peacefully
Drifting away.

Harry Horsfall, Knebworth, Hertfordshire

SCOUTS

On Wednesday I set out for camp,
For a little rest, for a total revamp,
We all had fun, we all played games,
I met new friends and learned their names,
My own went from "piglet", to "pixie", to "gnome",
And then came Sunday, it's time for home,
We all re-packed; the tents came down,
Out of the country and back to the town,
My memories of camp will last,
Even though it went so fast,
The boys at first I thought were louts,
But they're much better known as 6th Erith Scouts.

Eddi Newick, Thatcham, Berkshire

IN A HEARTBEAT

Full of wonder, love and praise,
I only have to look and gaze,
Out of the window, to look and admire,
And see all of the things that I so desire.

I should be grateful for what I've got,
And notice the wonders that I spot.
I've felt hopeless and worthless in my time,
But now I'm happy and full of shine.

I'm really content with my life,
And must not look for all life's strife.
Moments of joy and moments of sorrow,
Together they make up the days of tomorrow.

E Denham, Rickmansworth, Hertfordshire

ON THE TRAIN

On the train, looking out
People's faces roundabout
Scouring a paper, reading a book
Some not knowing where to look

Men are working, sorting clues
Women talking, sharing news
Some asleep, tired still
Me writing, as I will

Into London, as we go
Whereabouts, they only know
Me, a conference, at Westminster
Thoughts over which to linger

It makes a change, on the train
For me at least, something to gain
To spend special time, thinking
On the train, looking in.

Pat Wood, Welwyn, Hertfordshire

YOU

Living without you
I just can't do
Right here beside me
Is where you should be.
You feed the hunger
That comes from within,
You fuel the fire
That rages inside.
You mend all the bridges
Tear down all the walls.
Show me the light,
When there's nothing but dark.
You hold me together
When I'm falling apart,
You give me hope
When I see no end
Keep me warm in your arms,
When the cold's all around,
Swearing that we'll never part
Devoted love until the end.

Sharon Folds, Wheathampstead, Hertfordshire

QUAKE DANCER

The noon flickers in a painted thunderstorm
Fire dies
The air sapped and strangled
Her legs wrap around the bones
Her name escapes the dead wind

The light hums in her eyes
Wobbles like they're filled with tears

Arms flailing in grace
To maul the runes engraved upon the plain
Deep meanings through the black corridors
That twist the shadows round her
Calling beasts to scare her

Her eyes really filled with tears
She stops on one point
Her finish
The light black
The whispers grow onto her bones
Her name carried on the dead wind

David Kennedy, Newbury, Berkshire

COUNT THE LEAVES THAT COVER MY GRAVE

Count the friends that stayed when my grief became to
much
My sanity took a holiday at the coast
Me, Christ and Napoleon breakfast on burnt toast
So many left, so many ignored
The silly mad boy, whose only words for toys

Count the leaves the that cover my grave
Count the only friend who stayed

Count, count, count.

Tony O' Brien, Langley, Berkshire

THIS ARM

This arm reaches out across the sea,
This arm has so much love for thee.
This arm is long, this arm is strong,
This arm can never do you wrong.
When night is here
and long shadows creep near
This arm will guard you, have no fear
It can stop the wind and stop the rain,
And make small rivers run again;
It can crush mountain, build a town,
Pick a small baby from the ground.
When soft wind blows, from where, you don't know,
And you feel a gentle breeze upon your cheek,
It's only my hand that's trying to speak:
For this arm will worship you like none before
Till the day you open Heaven's door
This arm is mine.

R A Lane, Hornchurch, Essex

MIDNIGHT CAR CRASH

Over the Channel, almost home.
Coming up to midnight. In the car, alone.
Going down the by-pass. Only twenty miles to go.
Bright light in the distance, following the flow.

Or is it?

Getting ever closer. I'm unable to decide.
Is it in the traffic or speeding on my side?
Nervous just a little. Light looming ever larger.
Starting to feel anxious, aware of all the danger.
Huge light is now upon me, sounding like a roar.
It hits me like a steam train. Demolishes the car.
A black-clad drunken figure, helmet over handle bars.
The sound is like a shotgun. Body flies above the cars.
Car dies beside the roadside, others coming to a halt.
I climb out, mind in turmoil. French nightmare.

Drink the fault.

John Garner, Thatcham, Berkshire

John Garner said: "I am a primary school teacher and
have written verse for a number of years, initially as amus-
ing commentaries on teaching situations. My work is influ-
enced by news headlines, comic situations and personal
experiences. Writing has been for the amusement of family
and friends but this first publication may inspire a few
loftier ambitions. I live in Berkshire with my wife and
teenage daughter. I relax by watching football and would
love to meet Ray Pointer, from the great Burnley team of
the sixties. I spent time in France and 'Midnight Car Crash'
was inspired by a very personal experience during that
time."

FRIEND TO ME

Brother, uncle, friend to me
No task too great, too dark to see.
Gently waiting in the wings
To guide, support, forget our sins.
To love our children as his own
Yet live his life, content, alone.
How great this man who now is free
Brother, uncle, friend to me.

Alison Burgess, Newbury, Berkshire

This poem was written for the funeral of my uncle, Alan McLaren, and is dedicated to his memory.

GENESIS

Curling of the foetus in the womb,
Soft helpless embryo,
Creation within creation,
Dependent, absorbing life effortlessly
Until the sharp sudden thrust
Of the body to the world
Uncoils the tiny shape
And light strikes face and skin,
And eyes yet blind to see.

Green shoot of snowdrop
Pushing through the soil persistently
Symbol of fertility,
Rising toward the pale winter sun
Paying homage to its chosen god
Symbol of new life, of hope,
It spikes through the brown sludge.

Pauline Moulder, Castle Hedingham, Essex

TRUE FELLOWSHIP

The falconer's wings protect thee.
Thou shalt come to no harm.
I to thee show protection.
My mercy is indisputable.
Come celebrate with me the
flight of the falcon.
Flight upon flight of victory.
Unsurpassed beauty of wing.
Nesting, nesting so trustingly
under the falconer's wings.
Head high for heights,
see thy purposes come true.
Take the flight of the
falcon and I shall minister
to you.
Do not become worried and
apprehensive when you can be
truly alive and fly in the
Spirit of the falconer and
become my child at my side.

Anne Hadley, Langley, Slough, Berkshire

OCTOPUS

Deep beneath the sea, an octopus swimming free.
Glides along numerous routes,
Mimicking surroundings with accuracy.

Above, sunbeams dance and glitter (like the Northern
Lights).
But this octopus is undisturbed,
Finding contentment in its solitude, what an attitude!
An octopus is a lonesome creature.

If it sees a stranger, and is annoyed,
It escapes in a cloud of ink-whoosh! away it goes,
With the tide that flows, tentacles swinging to and fro.

An octopus that is big and fat, with suction pads (as on a
rubber mat).
Grey, like an overcast sky.
Crawls along the sea bed, slowly like a snail.

Tentacles creep, seeming inquisitive and uncoordinated.
Twisting and turning like the tendrils of a plant,
leaving a trail in the sand.

In an octopuses domain, sea fans sway.
Above, fish synchronize with the rhythm of the tide,
dancing, so it seems, as time goes by.

Sea life continues, and would not be the same, without an
octopus swimming free.

Sarah Weyl, Reading, Berkshire

THRICE JO, AND LUCIE

Performance night by "Soundhole" for a
harbour-shape of figures
arranged with open dancing-space,
that gradually is covered
by people still arriving
and settled at first notes.
Partly hidden dancers
are in the shadows of the hall barricaded
from the band, by the seated, silhouettes like boulders on a
beach
taking up in the middle-ground.
As light-house changing colour
splashes those who sit or dance in red then
blue-blending in a rhythmic sight and sound applied by
pipes and violin-guitar and special tambourine.
Young female world of four
linked in happiness together
slimly swaying with the tide
on line and semicircle drift into a square
and cluster of brief moment.
Vision of a male receives
the pointed shell they form
with him returning near the band
shadow to full beam
encouraging the rise of silhouettes to free the dancing
space.

Reg C H Baggs, Windsor, Berkshire

*Dedicated to Joanne Barber, Jo Coulson, Joanna Frost and
Lucie Maynard for their dancing inspiration, also to
Alexandra.*

TO SHARE WITH YOU THIS PLACE

I call out to you when I'm lonely
To help me through this space
I call out to you when I'm happy
To share with you this place

I call out to you from the garden
Amongst the trees and shrubs
I call out to you to share this place
With hanging baskets and flowering tubs

I call out to you in my sleep
Sometimes torture on my face
I call out to you when I'm awake
To share with you this place

To share with you this place
Is a heaven that's made on earth
To share with you this place
Fills my life with so much worth.

Pauline Waugh, Slough, Berkshire

A DOG'S REPRIEVE

I bit the postman for a lark
And then faced death row in the dock,
Protesting with a fretful bark:
'You know I'm not a criminal but
Britain's sacred animal.'
The postman in the witness box
Showed a man, 'His honour,' the marks
Of my jocularity who said, 'They look benign,
And laddie's tail is wagging, a friendly canine.
Unmuzzle and bring him over here.'
When I was taken near his chair
I raised my forepaws in the air
And on his knee them laid,
Then with his tie I played
As roars of rapture rent the forum
Briefly disrupting court decorum.
He ruled, 'Laddie shan't sleep in a mould
But be awake to delight the world.'
Bark of my best manner: 'Thank you, your honour.'

Walter Jennings, Cippenham, Berkshire

Walter Jennings said: "My desire to create beauty in words
was felt in youth when writing simple verse seemed not dif-
ficult. I maintained this hobby throughout my career as a
physiotherapist. I have written over 30 poems and had
seven published. I also write short stories and articles, win-
ning five awards. Born of British parents in British India, I
settled in England in 1979. I have been a member of the
Poetry Society for three years. I am now writing a novel in
verse on an Iranian marriage custom."

THANK YOU

I thank you for the time you gave
When everything was bad
Now that you are gone from me
I truly do feel sad
I know I have the memories
In a pocket in my mind
Buried deep inside of me
Often hard to find
I hope that we meet up again
In a distant time and place
I'm glad that you are happy
Keep that smile upon your face

A W P Poetry, Slough, Berkshire

VANITY

My vanity expresses itself in ways strange and silly;
It doesn't lie in personal preening,
My hair is combed un-mirrored,
But when you cease to smile
When you frown for lengths of time
Or drive at a constant and furious rate,
I think "What have I said, what have I done?"
You don't speak to me, you look ahead,
And I stand, sit, lie silent beside you.
When you speak it is an average remark
And I am amazed; it wasn't me,
It was something outside me that had touched you.
Impossible when I am all-important to you.
This then is my vanity,
Foolish, unnecessary and always there.

Linda Butcher, Laindon, Essex

HOLIDAY

Running the marathon of pension
Fund accumulation and workerholically
Stunned by the 65 full years of celebration,
Longing for pleasures of the joie de vivre turned to
The fin of life concentration, of the deprived and slaved
years
With work smothered damnation, you hit the town,
Now, with the zeal of a prisoner who's been out
On parole and found it.
Confounded may be the life that should have you
Grounded then and now, the sun has cooled down.
The dry skin shivers at coming winter's frown.

Katrina Day, Reading, Berkshire

THE OLD CHURCH

Sequestered in its tree the old church lies:
A monument of beauty that has sought
To soothe the soul: whose grey stone walls have caught
The sunlight from a thousand golden skies.
Here the still air of musty secret tries
To tell of vigil kept and battles fought:
Of miracle some halting prayer has wrought.
Born of despair and choked with stifled sighs.
Here are the shades of mingled smiles and tears,
Here have been care and aching worry shed,
Here in the dim, grey dusk of day one hears
The ghost of hymns with the long ages sped;
While, pressing close, regardless of the years,
Lie the quiet legions of the sleeping dead.

I Bates, Reading, Berkshire

COLLECTORS' FAIR

On Sundays in the local halls
Some goods are well displayed
They spread them out on several stalls
We're sure to be waylaid.

There's silver, glass and carlton ware
Pictures, clocks and gold rings
Meissen and spode, touch if you dare
Eyes on you in the wings.

Doulton's part of my collection
And hatpins made of glass
Stare at all with great affection
But not that awful brass.

To make an offer, wear a mask
Inside you're full of glee
Now ready to take on the task
Of showing the family

Angela Adams, Wokingham, Berkshire

ORIGIN

Boomer-boomer-boomerang
From the land of aborigine
With animals, marsupial,
Live bearing, young in frontal sacs,
Of kangaroos in open spaces
Found in far antipodes,
Where trees of eucalyptus grow
In that great land across the sea
And kookaburra and wallaby
Live alongside koala bears.
I now live where there's mist and rain
And summers cool and winters cold,
How I would love to go again
To where hot sunshine is the rule.
Boomer boomer boomerang
When hurled afar you will return,
Perhaps one day you'll take me back
To my birthplace for which I yearn
Where my December birthday falls
In summertime in far off Oz.

Marcelle Williams, Wokingham, Berkshire

THE SONG SANG

The song sat singing,
Softly singing on the sea.
In the throat's hollow
Sang the swallow.

The song sat swaying,
Softly swaying on the breeze.
In the whistler's word
Sang the bluebird.

The song sat sighing,
Softly sighing in the tree.
In the mother's love
Sang the dove.

The song sat sleeping,
Softly sleeping in the wood.
In the evening's hush
Sang the thrush.

Joan Humphreys, Wokingham, Berkshire

Born in Reading **Joan Humphreys** enjoys playing the piano, theatre visits, keeping fit, listening to music, reading and writing poetry. "I started writing poetry in 1996 to celebrate the golden wedding of my parents," she explained. "I was very much influenced by attending a poetry workshop at South Hill Park Arts Centre in Bracknell. I would like to be remembered as someone who has touched the lives of others for the good." Aged 63 she is a retired advisory teacher. She is married to Michael and has an ambition to publish a book of her own poetry. "I have written around 50 poems and had one published," she said. "The person I would most like to be for a day is an astronaut so that I could see the earth from space."

MY SEARCH

I put aside my last night dreams to face another day
For I had trod a stony path and stumbled all the way.
I held my soul in trembling hands, my body empty,
drained,
But where was God to take my gift, however badly stained?

Where was the light to blind my eyes, the ladder to the
sky?
Where was the cross for me to grasp as I prepared to die?
No gentle hand propelled me back, no glorious master plan,
So, as I draw my soul back in, I seek for God in man.

Marion Taylor, Thatcham, Berkshire

MY HAIRCUT

Hair like Clint Eastwood had it cut like this should, have
made me quite sexy, but I look like a hood.
All sinews and muscles his neck quite a size, my six pack
has slipped which is not a surprise, breath in to look thin-
ner, but what would be best is to eat much less dinner it
seems all's gone west.
In my mind I am eighteen or want to be still, instead I am
plus sixty and over the hill.
His arms are like oak trees, mine are looking more like,
Olive Oil's kneecaps, pitiful old tyke.
A transplanted body would be the best thing,
I'll see if I can't give my doctor a ring,
He said he might be able to give it a whirl,
He gave me the body of a beautiful girl,
Now that I have it I'll not be the same,
I'm out every night earning a bomb on the game.

Robert F Belchambers, Clacton-on-Sea, Essex

MY FIRST BIKE

The first bike that I ever had was bought
For me by my grandad

I saw it and I wanted it I cried and
Stamped my feet for it

I was barely two years old when
Grandad bought that bike for me

He bought it with his hard-earned wage
When Gran found out she had a rage

The cash was meant for something else
Just quite what I cannot say

All I really know for sure is that I got
My bike that day.

R C Preston, Rise Park, Essex

Dedicated to Frederick Thomas Furse RIP, grandad, father, husband and friend. Remembered always for your kindness, love and generosity. Your grandson.

Born in London, **Robert Preston** enjoys golf, swimming, DIY, and reading. "I started writing poetry early in 1998," he said. "I wrote my thoughts, memories of family and childhood times and my personal visions. My work is influenced by family history and life experiences and my style is thought-provoking. I would like to be remembered as both a realist and a dreamer." Aged 40 he is a police officer with ambition to be happy and enjoy life with family and friends alike. He is married to Jacqueline and has two children, Laura and Matthew. "I have written several poems but this is the first one to be published," he added. "I have also written an unfinished children's story."

MY LOVE

My love beams tonight
So just hold me tight
In my eyes you will glance
Then you make one advance
The music is lovely
So just let us dance.

With no care at all.
As we dance at the ball.
With you still in my arms
And the music has charms
What more can we ask
While forever it lasts

In our 48 years
We both shared our hearts
But with love still in bloom
And forgetting our age
Maybe one day
We will get on a stage.

R Collins, Windsor, Berkshire

I WALKED WILLINGLY

I walked willingly through darkness, from nowhere, across nothingness
until I found earth, stumbling as I went.
finding earth I learned to make flames, which replaced darkness with light.
But flames light formed shadows, devilish in their deceiving, fiendishly hiding the way forward.
So I fanned fires flames until they danced a lively polka
warming me and giving me a greater light
vanquishing scaring shadows, which pointed towards my fears despair and confusion.
The light of the world embraced me, like a long lost relative.
And encouraged me to explore.
Giving me faith, in which I have found a shadow free sanctuary.
In the silence of this sanctuary I hope to find my way back.
To that original darkness, to God and to a oneness with all of creation.
Where I shall be a separate entity no more.
Heaven. My journey's end. Call it what you will.

Paul Farmer, Reading, Berkshire

UNSPOKEN WORDS

Can you keep a secret?
There's something I'd like to say,
I sometimes feel beside myself,
My strength all washed away.

Can you keep a secret?
There's something you should know,
I sometimes feel an emptiness,
A space that doesn't grow.

Can you keep a secret?
There's something I'd like to share,
When you're lying next to me,
I'm so glad to have you there.

Can you keep a secret?
There's something I'd like to see,
Our daughter's face in heaven,
Smiling down at little me.

Can you keep a secret?
There's something I'd like to treasure,
A vision of baby Lacey,
In our arm's forever.

Joy O'Brien, Windsor, Berkshire

WEEPING WILLOW

When birds no longer have the strength to fly,
And the nightingale cannot sing.
When roses no longer have the will to grow,
And the world's lost everything.

When the willow no longer has the tears to weep,
And the stars refuse to shine,
When love birds no longer have the passion to love
And the cockerel crows at nine.

When the heart I have no longer beats,
And the words I write are not true,
Until all these afflictions should punish the world,
I'll still be loving you.

Stewart Harding, Windsor, Berkshire

Born in Ascot **Stewart Harding** enjoys playing the guitar, making music and playing snooker. "I started writing poetry when we had to compose a poem in my English class at school. I won, so it inspired me to carry on," he explained. "My work is influenced by inner pain and I would describe my style as words on an easel. I would like to be remembered as someone who was not afraid to do anything that they wanted to do." Aged 19 he is a bookseller with an ambition to write songs and perform them in a group. "The person I would most like to meet is John Lennon and my biggest fantasy is to play a gig at Wembley Stadium," he said. Stewart has written plays, songs, and many poems but this is the first one to be published.

RAIN

It never rains but it pours,
How true that saying is.
It rains, it pours, it floods,
And then it rains some more.

The news comes on,
Pictures of human pain,
Homes flooded, shops closed,
Animals marooned or drowned.

Cars and people swept away,
Families and pets rescued,
The kindness of man to man
The 'Dunkirk spirit' back again.

Where has this all happened?
Not on some foreign land,
Where monsoon weather is the norm,
But in Britain in endless storms.

Come the summer and the sun.
The water companies once again,
Will say "Save water now at once.
A drought is on its way!"

Sandy Rose, Kempston, Bedfordshire

GET UP

Take your troubles as you find them,
And they will soon take wing,
Let people think soon you do not mind them,
And they almost lose their sting,
Fate is always waiting for you,
No matter why, or when,
Maybe, someday he will floor you,
Even if he does, what then?
You get up, somehow,
Before the count reaches ten.

Ron Bird, Leighton Buzzard, Bedfordshire

HAPPINESS

What is happiness for you and me?
Is it being home with all our family?
When we put our key in the door
and shut the world out for evermore
Can it be a walk by the seaside
Watching the waves against the incoming tide?
Or perhaps a lovely summer's day
That seems to take all our cares away
Maybe it's in a baby's smile
That lifts our hearts up for a while
Could it be when that someone we love is near
Whom in our hearts we hold so very dear
There are many special gifts we hold in our hearts
That will never set us apart
For happiness lies within our soul
and until we can reach our goal
Our destiny will then be complete
We shall then have true happiness to keep.

Enid Skelton, Luton, Bedfordshire

THE NEARLY MAN

Have you met the nearly man
who almost always
nearly can?
His ideas and plans
never quite succeed,
what will it take,
what does he need?

Success for others he's
achieved
but himself somehow
falls short
when he never really
ought,
Perhaps he needs a
helping hand to come up
with a masterplan
then no more, the
nearly man.

R J Hayes, Luton, Bedfordshire

FROSTY MORN

The early morning countryside.
Looks like a giant iced cake.
The trees and bushes glisten
Ice sparkles on the lake.

Cobwebs along the hedgerows,
Like diamonds twinkle bright.
Each leaf, twig and blade
of grass
Shimmers in the early light

The red and gold of fallen leaves
Reflecting like lights in the sky
Jack Frost has been so busy.
Icing all as he went by.

A sprinkling of crystal icicles
Across our hillsides and the glade.
Giving everything a fantasy
That echoes winter's varying shades.

Nina Lenton, Roxton, Bedfordshire

SON

The first cry, heaven sent, relief.
Everything's fine, ten of each, fingers and toes.
Baby blue eyes, stare, focus, recognise.
My son. My mum.

Bonding strong, wondrous eyes latch on.
All to him; food, cleanse, comfort.
Helpless, clinging, special, life love giving.
Your mum. My little one.

Discover new each day; can, can't.
Doesn't matter, try again.
Slowly do it, take your time.
Grow so fast, not helpless for long.
Always will be, my son.

Suzanne J Webb, Luton, Bedfordshire

SUMMER NIGHT ON A HILL

The silence of a cloudless velvet night o'erwhelms me
Fitful points of stars, yellow bright, mine eyes see.
Alone, diminutive, but humbly proud in glory
That human mind is so endowed with power
To comprehend, though dimly, the breath
Of love and life and yet grimly to know death.

The evening breeze
Caresses the whispering grass,
Above in trees
The sighing zephyrs pass.
The silence breaks
My heart awakes
As with unruffled wings
A nightingale sings.

Douglas Darby, Dunstable, Bedfordshire

STRANGE LOVE

You turned me inside out with your games and even upside
down
Yet I wonder who played the fool last night?
and who, the role of the clown

For all I have left me are lonely nights
In a place
called heartbreak hotel
leaving you and loving you

In the way only you know so well

A Marshall, Melchbourne, Bedfordshire

SILENT TEARS

In her world there is no sun,
There's no pleasure and no fun,
There's no laughter and no light,
It's always dark, it's always night.
A rape of virtue, loss of trust,
It's so unfair, it's so unjust,
She stands alone, lost in a dream,
She knows she's dumb but longs to scream.
She used to dance, she used to walk,
She used to sing, she used to walk,
But she can't move and she can't speak
As silent tears caress her cheek.

Louise Searl, Maldon, Essex

IN SEARCH OF PEACE

Man's frail spirit plagued with doubts,
Encumbered now, with inner duties torn,
Yields with disquieting frequency,
To undue pressures, bravely borne,
So pursues with every good intent,
Those means to swiftly bring release,
Perhaps within religion's comforts seeks,
To find that rare and welcome peace,
To pacify his restless mind,
With teachings there his soul to overwhelm,
Or takes delight on some more earthly plane,
In nature's vast and glorious realm.

Roy Burton, Luton, Bedfordshire

GRAVES AT YPRES

Stunned silence as we walk up the rows
A field of white where red once flowed
Destruction engraved on the wall
Eerie silence marks us all

White slabs display your sacrifice
a simple tear will not suffice

I look to the hill where your enemies came
I look to your grave and read out your name

So young and forever young are you
of such horrors I never knew
Sent to die, sent to kill
Generations later, impact still.

Amanda Evans, Dunstable, Bedfordshire

NIGHT VISITOR

He walked into my bedroom
His eyes with love aglow
Stood silent by the doorway
Not sure if he should go.
He watched me stand beneath the shower
Eyes filled with love and awe
Our eyes met and he closer came,
Still wary, still unsure.
I climbed into my waiting bed
Picked up my bedtime book.
He looked at me again and gave
That loving longing look.
I felt his pressure on my bed
His hot breath on my gown
My arms went round his golden head
My dog and I laid down.

Yvonne D'Arvigny, Cotton End, Bedfordshire

*In memory of dearly loved little dog James, who shared my
bed for 10 years.*

A COUNTRY WALK

Warm is the evening sun,
as I stroll the country lane;
the cows graze quietly,
milked and let out again.

The blossomed trees give shade,
the leaves, like grass, so green.
Within the branches chants a chorus
from birds, chattering, unseen.

Wild flowers, mauve, pink and yellow,
peep out to form a wreath,
and, often so near the hedges
a stream ripples beneath.

The lane twists and is unending,
a path leads off to a hill.
Tracks are hidden, where sheep did venture,
seldom trodden, to be left so still.

Jane McLaren, Ampthill, Bedfordshire

THE FEELINGS WITHIN

The mind has to cope with many feelings,
Hearts that were happy, easily break in two.
Each time someone precious is taken from us,

Love of life seems to drain from you,
Often we think to back times we shared,
So many memories stay with us each day.
Some sad, some happy, but very special,

Of our loved one, who passed away.
For those of us who are now all alone,

An emptiness is left deep within.

Learning to cope with the grief we feel,
Our new life we try to begin.
Very hard it is,
knowing who to trust.
Each time a stranger faces you.
Dreams and plans which you made long ago.

One day with a new friend may come true.
Never will your loved one leave your mind,
Each day, in your heart, they'll remain.
Just knowing they're at peace, in God's tender care some-
day you'll be together again.

Josephine Nicolson, Dunstable, Bedfordshire

GERIATRIC GRAN

Her outer eye is rheumy: the inner,
sharp focused, frames worshippers at Wesley Main,
now British Home Stores. In buttoned boots and spats,
with flowered hats, the congregation rises.

Her outer eye zooms in; she sees a face,
smiles and in we spoon the geriatric stew,
(the half chewed gobbets wrapped in Kleenex).

"It's Jim's lad, gran." But, as we rise to go,
the inner eye pans round the varnished pews.
"And did those feet..." the organ booms.

Ken Clark, Bedford, Bedfordshire

MOTHER

I'll never forget my dearest mother
Who gave me birth, a sister and brother,
Nurtured me in my tender years,
Beside me thro' my laughter and tears.
Told me tales whilst I sat on her knee,
When ill, loving arms would comfort me.

I'll never forget my dearest mother,
Her foremost thoughts were for another,
Ready with kind words and deeds
To help with other people's needs.
She was my mother and my friend
Prepared me for this life to wend.

She greeted all with a happy smile,
Would find time to sit and talk awhile.
But now she's gone to a peaceful place,
No more shall I see her lovely face.

I'll never forget my wonderful mum.

Patricia Edwins, Leighton Buzzard, Bedfordshire

To Mum, who inspired this poem - a true portrait of you. Now at peace in tranquil Sussex beside Dad.

ODE TO EGGINGTON

Eggington, a place of peace,
Where countryside will never cease;
Where birds sing and flowers grow,
And people pause to say "hello".

Here's the church, all alone,
There's the hall, of local stone,
Countryside is everywhere,
With sheep and cattle grazing there.

Pretty houses all around,
The village centre they surround;
Owned by people old and young,
Here is space for everyone.

Oh, that everywhere could be
Such a pleasant place to see.
In this world of stress and strife,
Eggington's charm is its country life.

Jane Baker, Leighton Buzzard, Bedfordshire

Jane Baker said: "I have been writing occasional verses
since childhood and find it an ideal way to express my feel-
ings without going into much detail. This particular poem
was written for a Women's Institute competition and dis-
played afterwards in the village church. I have been
President of Eggington Women's Institute for the past ten
years, which has given me much pleasure. I am married to
Philip, and we have two children. We enjoy travelling and
have visited many countries together. 'Ode to Eggington' is
my first poem to achieve publication."

HAIKU TO THE MOON

Moonstruck lovers clasp
moved by forces savaging
tides and lunatics.

Patricia Crittenden-Bloom, Colchester, Essex

Patricia Crittenden-Bloom said: "Much of my poetry is drawn from nature, from the wilderness areas of Alaska and Colorado where I lived for many years. Retired now from the medical profession I am frequently to be found rambling the Essex/Suffolk countryside or poddling about in our small but vigorous garden. My work has been published in anthologies and literary magazine on both sides of the 'Pond' and includes travel articles as well as poetry. Currently I'm writing and illustrating a collection of children's stories enthusiastically encouraged by family particularly my grandchildren."

INSIDE EVERY FAT WOMAN

Thin is slim.
Fat is stout.
Thin is in.
Fat is out.

Though I'm fat
There is within,
Another me,
And she is thin.

The slim, thin me is
Always fighting
Through the fat me
To get out.
But fat is armed with cakes and chocolate,
So fight is always won by stout.

But with some help from willpower,
Victory might come from within,
And rout the spout,
And splat the fat
One day I hope slim thin will win.

Jean Stewart, Waltham Abbey, Essex

THE TOYS

The toys in the cupboard
had been waiting all day
when the children were sleeping
they' could come out to play
Tin soldiers would march
and the dollies would sing
The teddies & fluffy toys all would join in
they'd make tea and eat
using small cups & plates
and after they'd eaten
they'd play music tapes
they would then dance around
they loved night time the best
no one knew this went on
As the house was at rest.
they were all very careful
but if they were seen
the children would think
it was all just a dream.

E Summers, Romford, Essex

WATER RIDE

Lady's drifting
to the overgrown
finger name
unknowing the cold

Fluent break up
Playing the tune
of 3 chimes
carved in the rune

In nighted hours
a shaking house
an armoured fight
and I'm running out

Smile in the waves
here I am drinking
Two heavens have no name
and I too am sinking.

Michelle Hurley, Elm Park, Essex

OUR HEALTH CENTRE

They have built
a Minor Operation suite.

I think of Mozart, Strauss,
how might they sound
Vasectomy Minuet,
The Ingrown Toenail Waltz?

Nicolette Golding, Woodford Green, Essex

HUSBAND

What is a husband?

He's that lump in the duvet,
He's that crease in the chair,
He's that face in the corner,
He's that piercing stare.

He's the tears that I've cried,
He's the thoughts in my head,
He's the madness that strangles me,
He's the silence I dread.

He's the trap that I'm caught in,
He's my confidence broken,
He's the breaker of good things,
He's the words left unspoken.

He's the insanity that reigns
where normal life should,
He's the words that will kill me,
if only that could.

Angela Clapham, Romford, Essex

CONFUSED

Loving you but leaving you,
Wanting you and needing you,
Now I am so confused,
Because I am feeling used,

Am I loved? Or just my figure?
For my body? Or forever?
I need to know so I can choose,
Is this love? Or do I lose?

Erika McCusker, Stanford-le-Hope, Essex

UPON A SUMMER BREEZE

For when upon a summer breeze
the bumble bee, a bush he sees
to settle where he may
upon this bright blue summer day.

And whereby meets a butterfly
upon some lavender looming by
A blooming rose of bloody red
thrives from neath the flower bed.

And daisies scattered all around
across the vast green velvet ground
which quiver gently in the breeze
to compliment the rustling trees.

Then butterfly and bee together
they soak up the sunny weather
dancing bush to flower
as within an ivory tower.

Linda Monk, Chelmsford, Essex

GROWING OLD

The years grow cold, as you grow old,
When no one's here to share
I gaze around, and feel the chill
Of just an empty chair,
My thoughts then turn, to happier days,
When you were here with me
Those memories. still so warm with love,
Of days that used to be.

Miss you.

Joy K Halfpenny, Hockley, Essex

FREEDOM

I took one more puff on my cigarette
As I watch the clouds roll by
A sparrow landed in front of me
And without saying a word
I said to the bird
"I am human!".

I can go where I want
When I want
Think what I want
Do what I want
I have freedom

But as the bird flew off I thought
Do I?

Neil McBride, South Woodham Ferrers, Essex

*Dedicated to all who have supported me, but in particular
my mum, Brian and Chris, and my fiance Lisa. Thank You.*

THE DREAM

A gentle breeze carries me
on the wisps of cotton clouds
away from the violent back streets
away from the heaving crowds
I exist within a dream world
on the shores of an exotic sea
across an ocean of sapphire water
and a dream that beckons me
Solitude isn't loneliness
when on my island, there's only me
because I am one with nature
I'm a soul that's been set free.

Angela Barrett, Southend, Essex

NO, NOT YET

At the beginning of the end
I knew I would never forget.
Once in a while it might happen, I'd fail to remember, sweet
forgetness of passion.
How long does it take to get over a love affair.
If I think I am free, another memory comes along
seeking a place in my heart,
lasting for an indefinite time.
Then it slowly fades, leaving fragments to throw me off bal-
ance yet again.
Nostalgia strengthens the memories. Sweetens them, or will
increase the bitterness.
Is my past going to set me free?
It's going-going-going, no, not yet.

Helen J Cox, Basildon, Essex

MUMS

Mums are
artistic painter
big hugger
cake maker
child helper
fab photographer
funny joker
good looker
great cooker
Hairdresser
leaf raker
manic shopper
skillful gardener
TV watcher
warm lover.

Mums are just the best ever.

Priya Mistry, Colchester, Essex

Priya Mistry said: "I am 11 and I was born in Liverpool. I started writing when I was seven and I entered a Blue Peter competition called 'The Day Something Happened'. I was a runner up so I had my poem printed. Ever since then I've really enjoyed writing poems. Another thing that influenced me to write was that when I was nine I went to a creative writing course in Saffron Walden. It was great because everyone loved writing. There I met a great storywriters Stephen Bowkett, Peter Hayden and Jane Newbury. I enjoy writing poems and I hope you like mine."

CONNECTING PEOPLE

Benches to right, some to left;
They throng in harmony; Shopping bags knock together
Their owners sit down, chatting heartily.

The aroma from the hamburger stall erodes the air,
Customers chew their way through much favoured fare,
There is a bookshop next door;
Newspapers and magazines, galore.
Cassettes, maps and a whole lot more.

A chemist nearby; I venture in
Vitamin pills, lipsticks and cream for the skin.
Where are the corn-plasters? I asked the
assistant, with red hair;
Right near to the talc, just over there.

I will research, dressmaking and house decorating
But my first priority, is to fathom, the 'Know How' on wine
making.

A busker strums his violin, outside the post office,
I enjoy a moment of respite.
Mozart and Schubert to my delight; a clever chap.
I place coins into his well-worn cap.

Minnie Fenton, Waltham Abbey, Essex

TO THE LADY OF THE HOUSE

Oh lady of the house so fair
I love it when you brush your hair
I pine as you take sips of wine
Or can't decide quite what to wear.

I laugh when you tell off the cats
And use flower pots as plant cane hats
My heart just flirts as you iron my shirts
Or carry out the refuse sacks.

I sympathise when you get hot
Then offer jumpers when you're not
I'm truly smitten when you're bitten
By the urge to go and swot.

Oh lovely lady of the house
You really are the perfect spouse
I'll tell you even though you know
I love you and will e'er do so.

Ken Aldred, Colchester, Essex

WINTER

Pine trees bending with white weight
with boughs encrusted in its magnificence
the green melody silenced
softly sleeping until the spring.

Rivers stilled in their flight
silvered slivers of once liquid substance,
now silenced in suspended stillness.

The talent of the world
with its hand upon the crust
seeping coldness from the cracks of the orb,
now the earth rests.

J Booker, Colchester, Essex

RELEASED LIGHT

You layed directly under sunbeams
Follow the glistening mystical stream
Perfection in a room of white
Smell the magnolia pleasantly light
Floating of yellows whites and creams
Upon your windowsill are stars in a jar
As memories drift away so far
Comets collide and fireworks scream
Mists arise as heat causes steam
Your past has never left a scar
Towards the sunset you drive your car
Ride with me to a place of peace
Where ideas and feelings you can release.

Sarah Morgan, Harlow, Essex

CHILDREN KNOW BEST

Children of the world unite
Grow-up folks may like to fight;
But you have a much better way,
Boys and girls come out to play.

Children from Iraq and Kossovo
Are not concerned with who rules who
and Argentinian kids, I'm sure
Don't care who guards the Falkland shore.

And in far India's coral strand
The young play hopscotch in the sand
While under Greenland's icy peaks
They amuse themselves with hide-and-seek.

And round about the Cape of Good Hope
They twirl around the skipping rope;
In perm and Astrakhan no doubt
Calling one-two-three, you're out.

So teach your elders as you play
How to seize the present day
Not in war and suchlike madness
But in play-times joy and gladness.

Elsie Karbacz, Colchester, Essex

THE LAND OF PEACE

The meadows that I gaze upon,
of marshy lands far and beyond
the lands of high-rise building blocks,
standing round in cement like flocks.

The mellow smell of old oak trees,
whispering in the cool day breeze.
The herd of cows that chew the cud,
a pair of pigs wallow in mud.
The sheepdog barks to lambs astray,
the carthorse waits in fields of hay.
A mother swan protects the way
for cygnets who have gone to play.

And all about the sky is blue,
the grass is green, the flowers bloom.
Yes, I believe that all around,
Hope reigns within this promised land.

Linda Helm-Manley, Harlow, Essex

Linda Helm-Manley said: "I started writing poems when I
was about ten. My grandmother died and I couldn't express
how angry and upset I was, so I wrote my feelings down. I
have a collection of about 80 poems. None have been pub-
lished until now. A poem, I feel is a very personal thing yet
it is so very special when somehow in some way, it is
shared with another."

THE PRISONER'S WOE

That I am, Richard.
I am no king and cursed Bolingbroke says yea.
A deposed king, when abdicated thee
No life for I, but grave pit for me
I lay
Somewhat wanting, I fear
For my life to cease, I tread in despair
Haunted by the devil's fiend.

Anxiety throngs my brow
As this recreant overthrows my peerage
Hark on thou. To have the gaul
He answers in person, "Release the crown".
Failing a word hesitantly, he cross-examines me
Orders to unshackle the responsibility
Put pen to paper as one vows
Sovereignty dispossessed,
amid witness by all to see.

Rat-infested place, now kept
A dungeon besmirch of foul dead
For destiny changes its course, we dread.

David Lawrence, Harlow, Essex

LIFE AFTER KIDS

We've said goodbye to the hard life,
We've waved goodbye to the kids,
We've banished smelly nappies,
and chocolate covered bibs.

The start and end of school days
are now all in the past,
No more endless homework
They all have jobs at last.

Now there's just the two of us
To do just what we wish,
No need to lock the bedroom door
when we want to cuddle and kiss.

The washing lie is often empty
The iron is redundant,
But oh the joy when we look around
The cleanliness is so resplendent.

D E Flynn, Manningtree, Essex

LIVING BY THE SEA

It is the sound of the sea that galvanises me,
Whether it be a gentle swish or a rage set free.
All my life I have never been far
From the beaches where Neptune is pedlar.

It is an ominous being,
At once inviting, at once killing.
It never ceases in its flight,
With the moon its pilot through day and night.

Great men have weakened in its path
As it tests and teases with nature's craft.
No sure footing will it ever yield
To those who venture in her field.

And yet the terror of her ways,
Is the magnet for those who at her gaze.
It is a love consuming the consumed,
A love that's like a passion exhumed.

So when you hear the sound of the sea,
Respect and salute her carefully,
Then she may allow a short incursion
Into her kingdom without immersion.

Yolande U Clark, Clacton-on-Sea, Essex

Dedicated to Project Clearwater for cleaner beaches celebrating the achievement by Anglian Water when AMEC tunnelled 3.5km with 100% safety and three new world records.

THE PAST, THE PRESENT AND THE FUTURE

Is it children, is that why we're here? To keep creating life
until we disappear.
Years of education to learn nothing about life, hours of
exams that apparently map our future plans.
We start with nothing and end with nothing, and that's the
way it's supposed to be, so why do we bother with what's in
between?
There's no poem in the world that could describe the point
of life, all we can do is make it last, and remember that all
we'll have in the future is the past.

Ana Ahmady, Sible Hedingham, Essex

MAKE MY DAY

A blackbird singing at break of day,
Wakes me up, gets me on my way.
He follows me right down our street,
With cheerful notes oh so sweet,
My working day won't seem so long,
For other birds join in his song.
What a dreary place this world would be,
Were it not for the likes of he.
I work outside in the morning sun
Cutting grass till the day is done.
And when I go back home at night
He sings to me till last daylight.
We give to him his daily food
In exchange he lifts our mood,
It is but a small price to pay
To cheer our spirits every day.
What a sad place this would be
Were it not for the likes of he.

James Meek, Clacton-on-Sea, Essex

HISTORY

As an oaf indelicate,
I bruise you with my words;
you turn and spit
the bitterness of your past;
but, oh, my love,
how can I heal
when wherever I kiss
my lips brush wounds.

Michael Shearer, Ingatestone, Essex

MY GRANDAD

Your eyes so blue
Your skin so smooth
An unblemished crown of hair
And a rich sailor's beard frame your face
Your body frail, your mind so strong

A life well-lived, a great journey to life's end you did travel
The remembrance of your well spent life is so sweet
Your wisdom is the sunlight of your soul
Your legacy to the world is your well educated family
Taught by the greatest teacher we're ever know

Of thy sorrow be not too sad, for evening praises the day
Death the life
I love you all the love in the world and a whole lot more
So until we meet again goodbye
Forever and a day.

Paulene Coe, Harlow, Essex

WAR CHILD

I would like to be
In someone else's mind
To see what they think
To see what I could find

I would like to know
Their fantasies and dreams
I would like to see if they
Know what life means

I have no idea
My mind is blank
All you would find is an empty tank
Where bombshells hit
And dead people lay
Where there mind's normality
To be led astray

I would like to know
Before my death day
But no one cares
And it's too late to pray.

Brandon Penalver, Clacton-on-Sea, Essex

Brandon Penalver said: "Most of my poems are about
myself and other people that have made an impact on my
life. Poetry is the only way I can express anger or pain I
may have had for anything or anyone, a way of crying with-
out tears. This poem is about a boy who had a problem of
knowing the difference between right and wrong. He often
asked himself questions about life expecting answers, as if
he were two people. Numerous problems mentally scared
this child's mind. Nine years later he's just been able to get
his head straight."

THE DAFFODIL

Resplendent in majestic gold,
She stands erect and dignified,
Her petals unfurling one by one,
Her trumpet gleaming in the sun,
Proclaiming winter's reign is done.
And I wonder if with fragrance sweet,
She, our Lord, didst also greet,
On that first glorious Easter morn
When everlasting life was born?
And didst uplift her head on high,
Her trumpet pointing to the sky,
To herald, man no more would die!

Joan Carter, Romford, Essex

MAGICAL

Wind, rain and the cold
This time of year a tale is told
Known to young and old
A time of good cheer
Another year soon ending.

Send a card put a smile on a face
People rushing around, buying gifts
One gift has heaven a baby sent
Forget your troubles
A time of year to be happy.

Soon another magical year flies across the cold night sky
Bringing smiles to children
Its winter but, think on, its Christmas soon.

M Elliott, Barking, Essex

THE WANDERER

The countryside I know and love
Is alive with the warmth of spring.
A myriad flowers surround my feet
And in the trees birds sing.

I don my rucksack and my boots
And trek for miles
O'er fields and mountains and by streams
And clamber many stiles.

I love the peace and solitude
As I wander o'er hill and dale.
My heart soars upwards with the lark
As the fresh air I inhale.

From Sussex downs to Lakeland peaks
What beauty lies in store?
And as long as health and age permit
I shall wander evermore.

Audrey Wright, Romford, Essex

THE SECRET WALK

I stroll along a deserted beach
As the sun begins to rise.
The promise of a perfect day
With wonderful clear blue skies.

Just the gentle lap of tiny waves
As they break upon the shore,
No other sound to disturb the peace,
There's nobody here at all.

The sand so soft between my toes,
My thoughts can drift away.
A gentle breeze upon my face
How I wish that I could stay.

But no one will know
That I've walked this way,
Because whilst other folk sleep,
The tide will wash my footprints away
And my secret walk I can keep.

Pam Williams, Wickford, Essex

RENE

I'm 75 and you don't care,
I'm asking for help from anywhere,
Tell me where are all the authorities,
The council who looks after its properties?

The social services who are to help with peoples welfare,
They all get paid good money to show that they care.
I've tried my best for over fifty years,
Now all I have left are rooms full of tears,
I fought for my country in 1945,
My only regret is staying alive.

Wendy Gavin, Clacton-on-Sea, Essex

Born in Worksop **Wendy Gavin** enjoys music, reading and
writing. "I started writing poetry when I was 12 to put my
feelings and emotions on paper," she explained. "My work is
influenced by life itself and my style is meaningful and free.
I would like to be remembered as a little person with a big
heart." Aged 42 she is a mother with an ambition to pub-
lish her own book of poems. She has two daughters and
one son. "I have written short fiction for my children and
also over a 100 poems," she said. "I have had a few of my
poems published and my biggest fantasy is signing my own
books and donating some of the profits to charity."

LAKE DWELLER WOMAN

Looking onward to what she
cannot have but once possessed;
that sleepy heaviness,
the fruit of her ecstatic
but now
burden some labour,
such fleeting moments,
they pass and so too,
will the last ripple of the lake.

Carmel Belcher, Dagenham, Essex

TEARS ON MY PILLOW

Rain on the window,
Tears on my pillow,
My spirit bends
Like the wind-swept willow
'Neath the angry surge
Of your blistering ire,
Dampening the ember
Of my offered desire.

Rain on my heart
Tears a jagged split,
That all my entreaties
Yet fails to knit.
For the storm of your anger
Rages over my will,
And the tears on my pillow
Remain with me still.

Aleene Hatchard, Brentwood, Essex

INTRIGUE

Honey, you were seventeen.
And I was at the age of innocence-I was twelve.
Oh! it was too easy for me to fall into the trap of love.
But I felt it a blessing; a pleasure;
an indescribable emotion.
You came into my life and my heart
went from sugar pink to sizzling hot red
because you stabbed my breast with
the Dagger of Love.
You came into my life and a luminous golden light shone on
my face
revealing to me love's experience.
The light of your eyes touched my body
and the sky above me went bright red.
But you knew nothing of my constant gazing at you
whenever you were in my presence.
You played love's game with me
As if I was some porcelain doll,
But you can never go so far
that my love won't follow.

Nahid Zaman, Upminster, Essex

Dedicated to my precious literature teacher, Bruna Lamanna, who so faithfully and passionately believed in me and supported me.

Born in London **Nahid Zaman** enjoys creative writing, reading and working out. "I started writing poems at the age of nine, because I love to read and have so much interest in writing," she remarked. "My work is influenced by my innermost feelings, moral issues and also great writers. My style is free, spontaneous and flowing. I would like to be remembered as an unworldly, reticent and individualistic person," she said. Aged 19 she is a student with an ambition to become an economist. "I have written magazine articles on Islam and 30 poems but this is the first of my poems to be published," she said. "My biggest fantasy is to be a bold, dashing, daredevil, hellcat rider and a spirited, powerful, female warrior," she added.

SAY CHEESE

We're a happy bunch, at forty two.
Bringing smiles to all of you.
Catching moments, large and small.
And we'll send you a card, if you don't call.

From holidays, to weddings, we'll see you right.
And care for your photos, far into the night.
Our mini lab is second to none.
With hours and overnight all quickly done.

We'll share your tears and laughter too.
It's our pleasure to help you, every day through
But please remember, when tempers are fraught.
Good manners cost nothing, or so we are taught.

We always try to do our best.
Even lost photos, we'll make them our quest.
Rainy days, and sunny smiles.
Photos taken from across the miles.
But when things go wrong, it's up to us.
We'll sort your problems, with simply no fuss.

Janice Thorogood, Witham, Essex

DEMONS

In the chasm that fills my brain
The darkness is broken,
By small stars, dotted,
In their thousands
All racing upwards
At incredible pace.

A small tumbler filled with a dark liquid
Is held in the palm of my hand,
My fingers curving round it, encasing it,
Filled with the dream.

Swallowing the dark drink
In an inescapable consummation of
Fire and darkness.
I fall to the ground
Racing, in a flash of light
Up into the darkness.

Sarah Bidgood, Danbury, Essex

SIGHT SEEING BY METAPHOR

It is summer and the city is celestial.
Masculine buildings scraping the sky
Will be my furniture this September.
The river will wash me in its unfeeling caress
And my heart will burst with smog.
My adolescence places itself, misplaced,
In the city that never knew me.
The night bus tracks of tears
Blackfriars Bridge, August enemy,
Holloway road where I kissed her feet.
I stroll through my dreams
Touching without being touched.
Every station marks a teenage dream trampled underfoot.
The man, disorientated with age, wears a gaudy billboard;
It reads "Jesus is our Saviour." Etcetera.
London has secrets.
And she will die before she breathes a word.

Rebecca Dyer, Chelmsford, Essex

Rebecca Dyer said: "I am 19 and have been writing since I was very young, both poetry and prose, as well as for my own fanzines. I am currently studying communications and cultural studies at Goldsmith's College and my ambition is to see more of my work in print and possibly go into journalism. I write in order to capture experience, therefore my poems all have special meaning for me, but I hope that others can draw their own personal interpretations. Writing is my way of leaving my mark and is an integral part of whom I am."

IS THERE ANYONE OUT THERE?

This comes from planet Earth, a world full of strife
Yet full of wealth and plenty and the hopes of new life
Full of wars, suffering, disease and starvation
Scientific advancements
beyond our comprehension
An enigma, where men display cruelty to one another
Or acts of kindness to allow others not to suffer
We fear the worst if our actions persist
Let us know, if you can, does life here still exist?

David Evans, Weeley Heath, Essex

NEW BEGINNINGS

A new life begins,
As an old one ends,
The two just,
Don't seem to blend

I know I feel happy,
Although I'm rather sad,
Emotions are anything but bad

These feelings inside,
Are all part of a dream,
One I'm finding hard to believe

It will change my life,
In so many ways,
I hope I can cope,
From day to day.

Nina McLeod, Southend, Essex

SPRINGTIME IN THE COUNTRY

A duck glides by on a lake so calm
How could you imagine it would do you harm?
Maybe it wishes it could join the farm
Not on your nellie says my old maam

The flocks that we hold keep us quite warm
The noises they make aren't like the storm
If it's horses you want you can't sleep through the dawn
The trainer is up, so start mowing the lawn

In the back of the garden the gnomes are about
Enjoying their peace so please do not shout
The poor little imps that make up the scene
Of the suburban POP culture that is so serene

My brother's a teacher he shows children the way
His crop rotation brings a harvest one May
The exams aren't easy the bairns need to read
From tiny acorns big oaks from seed

As day turns to night the sun ever near
Obscured by the horizon, not a reason to cheer
With evening passed it's glow less a burn
Has dimmed to flicker, our moon demands its return.

Stewart Morton, Westcliff-on-Sea, Essex

Stewart Morton said: "I am a quiet person who doesn't like the company of loud or gesturing people and prefers the beauty of mother nature to parties and eating out. My hobbies are ambling, non-league soccer, national race meets, folk music, statistics and their analysis. My work is influenced by institutions I know well such as the Salvation Army, popular culture, populations size and destiny, prophets like Bob Dylan and of course my schooldays. I would like to be a journalist because all my mathematic proclivity was destroyed by them and they owe me a good turn."

FIRST OF SPRING

Sheltering from the April showers
camouflaged on budding bowers;
hearts in tune with beating wing
trembling claws on branches cling.

Wide-eyed they stare through fearful eyes
as rainbow darts transforms the skies.
With switched on sun, a lighting cue
the stage is set, their entrance due.

Hushed the whispering wind lies still
as babies mimic mother's skill;
comforted, they see her face,
and launch their bodies into space.

This annual play of life and death
that halts a heart and catches breath
reminds me that when on the wing,
baby bluetits start the spring.

Valerie Smerdon, Great Wakering, Essex

TRANQUILLITY

Oh, peace of mind
such calmness to know
how it rests me
how it chills my soul.

Turmoil in my brain
is at an end
peaceful thoughts, upon which
I can extend.

Peace of mind I have
thankfully I see
why can't I
like this always be?

Angela Humphrey, Colchester, Essex

THE BRAND NEW SHELL

We stood together, he and I,
Both of us trying not to cry,
Both of us being very brave
Gazing into an open grave.

He held my hand and quietly said:
"You know, my Grandpa's not really dead.
He's more like a crab, whose shell didn't fit
So he threw it away and got rid of it."

"Then wearing a shell, all shiny new,
He knew exactly what to do.
He went up to God in a different way
And I think that's where he is today."

Catherine May, Frinton-on-Sea, Essex

THE ABANDONED SHOP

In a shadowy back street,
Not lived in for years,
Is a shop that sells nothing,
But bad luck and tears.

The cash register's dusty,
And all covered in grime,
For this is a shop,
That is untouched by time.

The products are covered,
With mould and decay,
And some ancient baked bean cans,
On the dusty floor lay.

A black stain on the floorboards,
Made by a tear,
Is the telltale sign,
That death once lived here.

Tracey Pugh, Clacton-on-Sea, Essex

Tracey Pugh said: "I have been composing poems since I first put pen to paper. Although my parents have copies of all the pocms I have ever written, 'The Abandoned Shop' is the first I have submitted for publication. My vivid imagination was inspired by reading countless fantasy books and listening to fairy stories whenever possible. This has no doubt provided the inspiration for my work to date. I am 12 and have two younger sisters and attend the local secondary school in Clacton-on-Sea, where English is one of my favourite subjects."

THE BLACK PLASTIC BAG

The pavement is cold, I cannot sleep,
I spend my nights alone and weep,
You think I'm here by choice?
Well think again my friend
And listen to my voice.

My life is now in a black plastic bag,
A photo of Mum, a photo of Dad
And just for good measure I chucked in a toy
Just to remind me I once was a boy.

I had a home, a wife and kids,
Then the fatal day came
When I heard my name.
"You're no longer wanted we're sorry to say,
Pick up your wages at the end of the day".

I'm fifty years old,
Is that such a crime?
I'm afraid it it at this moment in time.
The cold slabs of stone are now my home,
No money, no friends and no hope.
I'm alone.

Teresa Turner, Clacton-on-Sea, Essex

US

As we stand by the ocean,
Our love clear to see,
We need no one else,
It's just you and me.

We'll pass all the ripples
And currents of life
With me as your husband
And you as my wife

The winds of change
Have no meaning to us
We'll just love long forever
No need for a fuss

As time will pass by,
A month, then a year,
I'll need nobody else,
As long as you're near.

Kean M Farrelly, Southend-on-Sea, Essex

Dedicated to Debbie Buckland, my heart, my inspiration.
Three words, eight letters, one meaning.

Born in Shoeburyness **Kean Farrelly** enjoys art, pottery, walking
and writing. "I started writing poetry at an early age," he said. "It
is a hobby passed down through generations of our family. My
work is influenced by my inner feelings and emotions and my
style is varied but to the point." Aged 43 he is a postman with an
ambition to have a book of poetry published. "I would love to be
the Poet Laureate for a day and the people I would most like to
meet are poets such as Keats, Shelley and Wordsworth to find out
what there inspiration was," he said. "I have written short stories
and 20 poems but this is the first one to be published."

SERENDIPITY

To hate. How wonderful.
Walking along her corridors,
Becoming a prisoner of her poison,
Free to feel her hatred running rampant inside me.

My only companions anger, loss and fear, they do not
relent they glow stronger year by year.

Slowly and quietly gliding on her belly,
She slithers through my soul shedding traces of her venom,
Like dusty grains of gold,
Each tiny little grain a dynamo of pain.

Seeping deep into my veins, breeding molecules of hate,
Until every fibre of my being cries out, you win, hate.
She is too powerful for my weakness,
Hatred becomes me, power replaces powerlessness.

On a path of grief and sorrow I am led to a vividly familiar
place,
Where I kneel and accept that my life's been cloaked in
Grace.

And in this garden of darkness and despair,
I believe the light will shine again,
And I will reach my destiny with gratitude,
For sorrow, loss and pain.

Caroline Mills, Loughton, Essex

EMOTIONS TURNED TO DUST

When your daylight merges into night
Search to find your leading light
It's out there waiting

When there is no one but yourself to blame
Release your guilt onto the flame
Feel the heat expelled

When you have nowhere to turn
Write down your feelings then watch them burn
Rid yourself of hatred

When you have lost your object of desire
Sprinkle your troubles onto the fire
Just learn to let go

When life becomes too intense to handle
Burn it in a lighted candle
Watch the ashes fall
As your emotions taper softly
Into dust.

Amberley Worton, Frinton-on-Sea, Essex

CHRISTMAS TIME

I see the snowflakes gently falling,
Outside my window pane,
Spring, summer, autumn's gone,
It is wintertime again.

The rooftops they are covered
Pure white with falling snow,
Children sleeping peacefully, dreams
Dreams of long ago,
Of Santa and his reindeer
Wondering how they know
To each they leave their presents
As house to house they go

Soon it will be Christmas,
Children shouting and smile with glee,
Windows bright with fairy lights,
Presents around the Christmas tree.

Their hearts filled with gladness,
As presents they unfold,
Once again all over the world,
This Christmas tale is told.

L Anderson, Colchester, Essex

CELEBRATE

Two thousand years;
Since he came.
Our saviour,
Lord Jesus his name.

He was sent to us,
From his father above,
To teach of forgiveness.
And of love.

As he lay in the manger;
On that night,
His head was surrounded;
By a light.

The light was the spirit,
From within,
Which will surely,
Wash away our sin.

Dorothy Lawrence, Frinton-on-Sea, Essex

UNTITLED

Awaken the sleeper
For the slumbers too deep
Awaken the sleeper
This time we play for keeps

Awaken the dreamer
For the dreams are so bad
Awaken the dreamer
Don't ever be so sad

Awaken from the nightmare
For things do get better
Awake from nightmare
Know I'm waiting for you

Paul D Walker, Upminster, Essex

Born in London **Paul Walker** started writing poetry about two years ago. "It was just about the same time that my marriage started to break down," he explained. "My poetry is influenced by my feelings and my style is morbid." Aged 30 he works in information technology and his ambition is to be happy and settled and also to have an impact on his son's development. "I have written over 200 poems but this is the first one to be published," he said. "I would love to meet Steven King so that I could find out how he actually manages to write all those books and the person I would most like to be for a day is Richard Branson," he added.

MY SON

When you're away oh how I miss you so,
I understand that you had to go.
You'd been so let down, but life goes on,
You really will recover from this son.

I'm always here for you, you know,
There's lots of places to see and go.
I hope you find what you've been looking for,
I'm sure you will find love and more.

While you're away son I will think of you,
You are my only son, I love you Stu.
So just for now do what you can,
Cause you're my all grown up young man.

We have a special bond it's true,
That's why I think the world of you.
So just be careful, safe and good,
Have fun, enjoy life as you should.

When you come home all safe and sound,
And when your plane is on the ground.
I'll be here waiting for you son
Because I have missed you, love mum.

Lesley Dearman, Holland-on-Sea, Essex

PRAYING TO MY LORD

I went into my church today
I said, my Lord I've come to pray
I saw a tear form in his eye
And then a really heavy sigh
He said I am always here for you
But there are just so very few
Who come to me and spend the time
And tell me what is on their mind
I love you all so very much.
But you just will not keep in touch
How do you think it feels for me
When my children I rarely see?
All I ask is how you are
You know I am not so very far
I can do so much for you,
In each and everything you do
Because I love you.

Fred Ablitt, Southend-on-Sea, Essex

I dedicate this poem to God, my inspiration.

Fred Ablitt said: "I have been writing poetry for approximately two years. I am a plumber by trade. I felt inspired to write poetry after helping one of my sons with his school poetry homework. Since then I have written over 150 poems on varying subjects. I would like to think my poetry is simply inspiring, enjoyable and humorous. My poetry is influenced by my Christian faith and everyday life. I am married to Julie and we have six children. My life is centred around my family and my Catholic faith."

WASTED

To watch and yet not see
To listen and yet not hear
To touch and yet not feel
To live and yet not know

Natasha Oakley, Clacton-on-Sea, Essex

LOVE

I thought this love so deep in me
Would never ever stray from thee
I had no thought to share my heart
But deep within I'm torn apart

I lay by you and think of him
And close my eyes to relive again
I made a choice but little knew
I'll love another as I feel for you.

When night's so still you touch my lips
My lonely heart cries for his kiss
I cannot take leave
And will never choose
I could not live to see who'd lose

And yet from his love
There's no will to part
His eyes light a flame within my heart
And with all to lose and nothing to gain
Again my life I'd do the same.

John Moore, Clacton-on-Sea, Essex

UNTITLED

I sit here looking out to see
What someday shall become of me
The day is young and so am I
What a feeling it would be to fly
High above the world I'd be
With nothing below but land and sea
What a pleasure, what a treat
All the places I could go and meet
The darkest of countries, the lightest of sun
It's such a crazy world to where I began
In the distance like a dream
All the things I could have seen
So I'm finished but so man made
So many secrets are left in the shade

Sarah Nelson, Little Clacton, Essex

THE VISIT

I went to the farm today Mum,
We all had a worksheet to do,
We looked at the cows and horses,
And Jonathan lost his shoe.

It bucketed down with rain Mum,
Our boots got covered with mud,
Miss Hathaway said "Be careful,"
As we splashed around in the flood.

My worksheet dropped in the bushes,
I explained when we reached the yard,
Miss didn't like my excuses,
And put a black mark on my card.

Sandra Watson, Leigh-on-Sea, Essex

MY FATHER

There in my heart, the still heart
I carried you,
I thought you were gone, gone forever,
But I held you
In my very veins.
In my eyes the colour of you,
In my blood the blueprint of you.
I carried you
In the dark curls
Of my child.
In everything I'll ever be
Reminds me of you.

Clare Collins, Burnham-on-Crouch, Essex

WHAT IS POETRY

Perception because of strange allure
Stirring deepest feelings,
verbally expressing
beauty of sound and sight.

The use of words
soulmates of the senses
to embellish, to enrich.
Like music depicting
the wonders of nature.

It's painting a picture
of all creation
it's sharing of thought
it's revelation
It's poetry.

Daphne Young, Clacton-on-Sea, Essex

CONSIDER THIS

Just look around at the trees and the flowers,
smell the air after the spring showers,
see the dew on the morning grass,
feel the sun shining through a pane of glass.

And I have to say how lucky I am.

Just look around at the rich autumn leaves,
smell the crisp air of a winter's night freeze,
see a white sheet of frost on the ground,
feel the cold air blowing all around.

And I have to say how lucky I am.

How lucky I am to wake up each day,
and feel and see what is in store for me,
How lucky I am to feel and see,
what God has created just for me.

Teresa Wood, Billericay, Essex

Born in Basildon **Teresa Wood** started writing poetry five years ago. "I wanted to encourage a friend who was going through a difficult time," she explained. "God is my inspiration and my style is plain and simple. I would like to be remembered not only as a wife, mother and friend but as a faithful servant of God." Aged 33 she is a housewife with an ambition to see more of her poetry published. She is married to Mark and they have two daughters and one son. "The person I would like to meet is Sir Cliff Richard. Despite his fame and celebrity status he has the courage to make a stand for what he believes in - Jesus Christ," she added.

KEYTHOUGHTS

Early in the morning, ere the birds awaken
The dew-washed foliage glistening white
Softly but clearly, keythoughts are spoken
Into my head. A hymn or a text.
Guiding my day. I know not the next.

Sometimes, twice only, the angel choir sang
A glorious crescendo of triumphant song
Wonderful joy and peace to bring
to one small soul.

G W Howe, Romford, Essex

Grace Howe said: "I have been writing verse occasionally since my late teens. I am 93 and a widow, with three married children and six granddaughters and two great-grandsons. I enjoy reading, writing and gardening. I have had articles, poems and a book called 'Thoughts By Grace' published by my local church."

THIS IS LOVE

What is love? they ask.
I answer. This is love.
A deep devotion born of each
And when life deals its bitter blows, two rending
Sobs in one great lurching sound
Two minds with but a single train of thought.
Two human hearts with but a single beat

When life its bitter lash doth wield, or,
Happiness its perfumed flower let fall.
Two minds and hearts, in perfect rhythm, interweave
Two human forms, with but a single soul
Residing in a world apart
This is love.

Irene Robinson, Dagenham, Essex

Dedicated to the memory of my late husband John Thomas Robinson, whose love for mankind, reached out to all.

THE SIDES OF LOVE

Holding onto the sides of love,
with my nails bleeding, as they start to crack,
I scream with pain, I don't want to fall,
Into the mire, of lovers lost fire.

As I slip down your beautiful body
to a darker place
all my grips are lost
as you fade from my face.

It's so cold, in this loveless room
with no windows, no doors,
no hope of escape,
bleeding heart that drowns in blood
and all fades from eye,
as life ebbs away I open the wrists of freedom,
on this cold day.

Clive Measey, Aylesbury, Buckinghamshire

AUTUMN

Although 'tis sad to see the end,
of glorious summer days.
Utter not a word against,
the following autumnal ways.
The wind doth blow and it may snow,
leaving you with red faces,
Underneath the ground there lies,
a host of dormant species.
Many of them cannot be born,
until the spring is here,
Now how are they to do that,
if autumn doth not appear?

Pauline Ilott, Oxford, Oxfordshire

SOMETHING ELSE

It scares me to think
I used to know
How to make you laugh.
Yet now through loss
Or something else
I can't even raise a smile.

I'd love to know
What's going on
Behind that same face.
Same but changed
Or something else
It's now different underneath.

Jessica Salter, St Giles, Buckinghamshire

ANNIVERSARY

This day is yours both past and present,
And you look back with pride on the years gone by.
The weary and the bad times add flavour to the pleasant,
They are merged and the memories of them are sweet,
Though you may wonder why.

Love will thwart the hardships in this life,
You will perceive wherein your loyalties lie,
With kind words of friends in your trouble, grief and strife,
You are not alone. Friends will be there to guide,
And troubles swiftly fly.

The future years may come and go,
But you look ahead with faith,
No matter what the weather,
Love will survive the heavy storms and sorrows that o'er-
flow,
Joy will be with you, for this day is yours   tomorrow and
forever.

Doreen Bowers, Waterlooville, Hampshire

FAERY HILL

I have found my home at last,
It speaks to me of ages past,
Of life and love and war
And hammering upon the door,
That shields the hearth within
From all elemental sin.

Grey lichened stone of old,
You are anything but cold.
I feel your aching pain,
You will rejoice again.
Left alone too long you crumbled,
Nevermore lie poor and humbled.

Your heart will throb once more,
Your spirit will awake and roar
From its slumbers deep,
After years of dreamless sleep.
Decadence will lose the fight,
Your empty gaze regain its sight.

M Mayes, Holland-on-Sea, Essex

JUDGEMENT

Warning signs across a gate
Two policemen stand before
Judgement on every animal's fate
Death decreed by law

Men arrive to execute
A swift final ending
Instructed to be absolute
Leaving nothing pending

Dumped into a mighty ditch
A hastily assembled pyre
Longer than a football pitch
A countryside on fire

Pungent smell of bodies burning
Palls of smoke exhaust
Clouds a deathly hush returning
To this rural holocaust

A Day, Luton, Bedfordshire

WHERE DO BABIES COME FROM?

I've just come back from hospital
To visit my dear mum
She's just had brother Michael
Dad says he came from her tum.

I really can't believe that
I think he must have lied
With all those cakes and sweets she eats
There'd be no room inside.

S Bates, Harpenden, Hertfordshire

SPRING PERESEPHONE

Spring. She is the season in two parts
The growing seed, the purest heart.
The vital grain that ever feeds
The earth and all mankind now needs.

Alive and potent, yet so mild
She gently nurtures nature's child.
The corn, the wheat, the fruit and flowers
She endows with all her powers.

Yet soon she will fast fade away
deep underground her part to play.
She procreates with every breath
Goddess of generation and death.

M Johnson, Reading, Berkshire

BEAUTIFUL THINGS

The world has many
Beautiful things like
Diamonds and pearls and golden rings. There's
flowers in bloom, the birds
that sing and the beloved rose of ours.

there's crystals that shine in the daylight,
and the shimmer of water
in the sunlight, but the most beautiful
sight in the world to me is the smile on your
face and your heart full of glee.

Constance Cullen, Watford, Hertfordshire

THE LADY OF SHALOTT

The river she shrouded like a large overcoat.
Longing to be near the castle tho' before her stood the
moat.
Inside was her lover with another was he.
Her own hatred she scorned for this woman unknown,
seated in the place of her wondrous throne.
Such glory was to be had if only to have him.
Tho' her brightness she was losing,
her white light had become dim.
No flags were flying, no drawbridge undone.
Just the reflection of her misery,
When out crept the sun.

Rebecca Wilkinson, Ware, Hertfordshire

LOVE'S CANDLE

Love can be like a candle, sometimes it's hot, then it's cold.
Love's not just for the young, it's also for the old
Love can creep upon you, when you least expect it to.
Love can make you happy or leave you sad and blue.
Love is always there in everything we do.
You're always thinking do I love him?
He's saying he loves you.
Love puts you in a whirl,
Churns you up and down inside
Love can make you want to dance and shout.
Love can make you want to hide
Love is like a flame, it blows about
Love is not always at home, sometimes it moves out
You will know when it is right
You will not be able to sleep at night.
He will say forever be mine.
And love will burn like a candle
A beautiful light of love to shine.

Trudie Sullivan, Oxley, Hertfordshire

HOLIDAYS

Holidays are fun
They make you very happy.
There is never one
Coming in a hurry.
Holidays are fun
Even though they make you tired.
They are always coming,
But never in a hurry.
Holidays are spread throughout the year,
There is never one without some cheer.
Sometimes they are long and sometimes short,
But you never get bored there's plenty to do.

Samantha Rodwell, Colchester, Essex

I NEED A DIRECTION

So afraid of failing
Afraid of rejection
I need a direction
What is meant by introverted after all
A parody of self absorption
I have an energy an anger to exhaust
Unaggressive out of shyness and not of thought
Quiet and reflective
Or disquiet and inactive
Negative and without motive
Where will I be in ten years time without a   direction?
Hope in my past, but that is what I am escaping
I need to look into the future with positive anticipation.

Simon Arms, Leighton Buzzard, Bedfordshire

SCENT OF A FRIEND

Any day fair or not so fair
You are one of the loveliest
flowers in my garden.

Any time, anywhere
Your bloom will surround me
Blossom fragrant sweet.

Debby Barnes, Thame, Oxfordshire

UNTITLED

Love knows no limits or boundaries
With love in my heart
I can say
With each passing day
Love grows stronger
and you get pulled in
When it pulls on your heart strings
With such a force
it sweeps you off your feet
and makes you complete
and happy inside
you are totally ecstatic with delight
and it makes you feel as though you
can fly and shout
and run around with a gleam in your eyes
full of surprise
you can see it in your eyes
staring back at you,
you will see it too.

Sharon Brown, Headington, Oxfordshire

ROM Q 2 U

Sitting in Kew Gardens
Breathing in the heady smell
of overfragrant rhododendrons
Plunging face into flower's scarlet throat
Then sudden sneeze
As pollen explodes from my nose

I think of you
Immediately wish I hadn't
What?

William Turton, Welwyn Garden City, Hertfordshire

BE MY VALENTINE

Eating is a pleasure,
when shared with you.
Singing and dancing is so good with you.
Friends that care and make memories to share,
could be me and you.
A cuddle is a human need of you.
A passionate kiss, turns me onto you.
A bite on the neck is a sexy thrill,
if done by you.
Touching your soft skin, makes my heart sing for you.
Making love is heaven with you.
Life can be so good with you.
My Valentine.

C Taylor, Didcot, Oxfordshire

longing

simplicity
stripped back
pared down
bare necessity

a lost art

Lynn Williamson, Kempston, Bedfordshire

LOVE

love is wonderful love is fine
love is feeling your hand resting in mine
love shines through in a baby's eyes
or a rainbow that appears in the sky
love is there all around
and gives you comfort when you're feeling down
love lights up my soul when you're standing there
love is when I know that you always care
love is a smile when its been a bad day
love is a mother who wipes the tears away
love is a feeling deep in your soul
love is there when you feel
you have nowhere to go
the greatest gift we have is love
it is sent to us from heaven above
so send out your love
let it flow from the heart
and give our world a brand new start.

Mary Barrett, Andover, Hampshire

GHOSTS OF THE FUTURE

Here we sit in solemn stillness
as of an age-old hymn
contemplating what is, what was,
what might have been.
Memories of yesteryear
flood the mind
like flashbacks from a favourite film.
Opportunities taken, opportunities missed,
opportunities to come;
that the past, so hauntingly reflected in the present,
may make way for the ghosts of the future.

Jennifer Chambers, Reading, Berkshire

VENUS IN DISGUISE

That lovely gaze where every eye doth dwell,
Like pools so deep and yet so crystal clear
That flowing blonde hair, so vivid, yet so fair,
That divine sweet voice even birds stop to hear.

Her physical beauty, though 'tis truly sublime,
Is surpassed by her wit and manner, a shy
Yet cheerful disguise, that makes you wonder why,
Fortune hath favour'd you o'er other poor fools.

From my blissful slumber, I suddenly awake
I once again lie in my chamber alone.
I feel sad and grave as I recall, a dream
It must have been but no more real have I known.

For you see, 'tis my problem, to my regret
Venus in human form, I have not met.

Christopher Lee, Wallingford, Oxfordshire

SUMMER HAS BEGUN

Cotton wool clouds in a baby blue sky,
Leaves gently sway as a breeze passes by,
Rows of terraced houses drowsing in the sun.
All is clean and shining now the summer has begun.

People wearing smiles after winter's cold
Young ones are playing, he's quieter for the old
They think of summer past when all was still to come.
The summer has begun.

Pam Farrer, Southend-on-Sea, Essex

Dedicated to staff and friends at the Queensway Activity Centre, with all my love and thanks.

LOST

It shone and glittered through the trees
Tantalising, yet beckoning
I stumble on
Bramble and thistle catch at my skirt
They hold me back.

Rainbow colours dance before my eyes
Exhausted I reach the summit of a hill
As sunset streaks the evening skies
The final rays linger still
Guiding me forward.

A golden glow played on a window far below
The village church stood silent, solid
The scene before me, peace
Some force I sensed had led me home.
I said a prayer.

Vera Saunders, Thatcham, Berkshire

OH, NO NOT ANOTHER POEM ABOUT A DOG

The main thing about my dog is how much I love him.
Do dogs understand that? I hope not.
If he knew how beautiful I find him,
How total my enslavement,
He might run off without me,
Not come to my call,
Do his own thing,
Be his own dog.

Less humiliating if he makes some show of compliance,
The odd "sit" or "stay", an occasional "roll over" on request.
We both know it's only courtesy,
Like children in a well-behaved class obeying their teacher.
Both parties acknowledge the rules, understanding the
game,
Choose to play it
But as for the cards
He has them all.

J F Marshall, Thatcham, Berkshire